SONG
OF A
NATION

SONG

THE UNTOLD STORY OF

OF A

CANADA'S NATIONAL ANTHEM

NATION

ROBERT HARRIS

McCLELLAND & STEWART

Hardcover edition published 2018

McClelland & Stewart and colophon are registered trademarks of
Penguin Random House Canada Limited

Library and Archives Canada Cataloguing in Publication

Harris, Robert, 1948-, author
     Song of a nation : The Untold Story of Canada's National Anthem /
Robert Harris.

Issued in print and electronic formats.

ISBN 978-0-7710-5092-3 (hardcover)—ISBN 978-0-7710-5093-0 (epub)

ML410.L32H32 2018   780.92   C2018-900577-7
                                           C2018-900578-5

Library of Congress Control Number is available upon request

Book design: Lisa Jager
Typeset in Dante MT Pro by M&S, Toronto
Printed and bound in Canada

McClelland & Stewart,
a division of Penguin Random House Canada Limited,
a Penguin Random House Company
www.penguinrandomhouse.ca

1 2 3 4 5   22 21 20 19 18

Penguin
Random House
McCLELLAND & STEWART

To Cassie, forever

CONTENTS

ACKNOWLEDGEMENTS

I FIRST CAME ACROSS the name Calixa Lavallée in 1976, when I was studying music at the University of Ottawa. A fellow student had become fascinated by Lavallée and his story, and my friend's enthusiasm for the composer was infectious. So I took out of the U of O Library the one and only volume at the time about Lavallée's life and music, *Calixa Lavallée: musicien national du Canada*, by Eugene Lapierre, originally written in 1936, and revised in 1950 and 1966. Based on the information in that volume, I wrote a couple of items about Lavallée for CBC Radio around the time "O Canada" was made our official anthem in 1980.

I must thank Doug Pepper and Scott Sellers at McClelland & Stewart for my renewed interest in Calixa Lavallée, almost thirty-five years after I first encountered him. Doug, my fine editor, told me that I would discover many new things as I worked on the book, and he was right. Some of them were about Lavallée himself, but more were about the Canada and Quebec of the mid- to late nineteenth century. I realized, to my shame, how ignorant I was, as an English Canadian, of the French Canadian interpretation of events that are as central to our country's history as Confederation and the Rebellions of 1837 and 1838. Lavallée's life and career, and especially his composition of the tune that would become our anthem, is completely tied up in that history—they are essentially inseparable.

I would also like to thank others at McClelland & Stewart for their work on this book's behalf, including Kimberlee Hesas, the managing editor; Lisa Jager, the designer of both the interior and the exterior; and Shannon Parr, whose help keeping track of changes was greatly appreciated. And Jared Bland, the publisher, whose support of my writing and this book has been unwavering.

My daughter, Dory Carr-Harris, from her perch in New York, has been tirelessly enthusiastic in encouraging me in this project, perhaps because, for the past year or so, she has had a ringside seat at the spectacle of a nationalism gone sour.

Finally, to my patient wife and dear companion, Cassie, my deepest thanks and gratitude for her ongoing support during this endeavour. I always feared that the next version of the anthem I played for her from my laptop, at full volume, was going to have to be the last, but it never was—her enthusiasm for the tune and the topic never flagged.

INTRODUCTION

WE ALL KNOW THE FEELING. A slight unexpected constriction in the throat. Heat rising to the face. Tightness in the chest. Tears—tears!—welling in the corners of our eyes.

We're responding, once again, to our national anthem. To "O Canada."

Maybe we're watching the Olympics, seeing our flag triumphantly ascend to the rafters in a stadium or pool or velodrome somewhere in the world.

Maybe we're in some high school auditorium before a holiday concert, listening to an enthusiastic, if struggling, student band.

Or celebrating with people from all over the world, surrounded by their friends and relatives, as they navigate the anthem minutes after receiving their Canadian citizenship, singing the tune shyly for the first time as Canadians.

"O Canada" touches us when our sense of pride and place and identity connect, and it creates in us a patriotic reaction that can burst out unexpectedly, for no reason—or for so many reasons.

We're not entirely sure what to make of our patriotism in a modern, cool, ultra-connected, digitally expanded world. It seems somewhat out of step with the current ethos, something artificially manufactured to sell us a certain brand of political product. And it frightens us when we encounter it too baldly. We know from experience, ours and others', that the nationalism that follows that patriotic pride can wrench some of the most destructive elements imaginable out of the human heart. Nationalism and civility, nationalism and peace, nationalism and reason, are often bitter enemies.

Yet there it is—that pride and that love and that joy in community that the anthem brings us. It means something. Exactly what that might be, we have spent a couple of centuries on this desolate and beautiful stretch of the planet trying to figure out, but our inability to do so doesn't mean there's nothing to discover. Somewhere deep in our collective experience, as we reflect on our past and contemplate our future, there is a psychic reality that deserves respect, a nub of a feeling for each other and our country that is powerful and demanding. Our anthem is just part of that psychic topography; it may not be its most profound aspect, but because of the joyous and childish pleasure that music creates in and for us, it has a special place in our national heart.

"O Canada" has been the song of our nation, working its steady way into the hearts and lungs of the population, for almost a century, although it did not become our official national anthem until 1980. That's not as unusual as you might think. "The Star-Spangled Banner" didn't get official status until 1931. "God Save the Queen" has never officially been proclaimed Great Britain's national anthem. Anthems the world over, because of their combination of emotion, politics, history, and symbolism, have long been objects of controversy. And ours is no exception. Nearly a century and a half after it first appeared, we're still arguing, often heatedly, about its appropriate English lyrics.

But where did it come from, this piece of music that affects us so? When was it written? How did it come into the world? How did it work its way into our collective imagination?

Most importantly, who wrote it? Who is the person who put our country's essence into song?

Meet the most important Canadian you've never heard of: Calixa Lavallée, a man whose life story might have launched a thousand movie scripts, or a dozen TV dramas. In any other country, one is tempted to say, he would be a near-mythic figure, swashbuckling and irreverent, affected with a wanderlust which propelled him across North America and across the sea. He was a composer, a performer, an entrepreneur, an educator, conversant with popular music and classical music—and he appeared in his quasi-colonial society, tragically, just ahead of his time. He left home at twelve, worked as a blackface minstrel travelling throughout the United States, fought in the American Civil War, was wounded at the battle of Antietam, produced the first opera in Quebec, wrote two of his own, became a leading figure in American music, journeyed to Paris to study for two years, tried and failed to create a Quebec national conservatory, and died in exile in the United States. And wrote our national anthem.

The story behind the composition of "O Canada," along with the story of Lavallée himself, is essentially a mystery to us because it has long represented the great taboo of our country, the wound we constantly try to mend or hide: that we were founded by French and English cultures in this country, to say nothing of the Indigenous cultures that lay behind both. Our understanding of ourselves will always be incomplete if we repudiate that cultural history or simply ignore it. So, the reason no one can be certain of the English words to "O Canada" is that there are no English words to "O Canada," or at least there weren't any when the song was written. "O Canada" wasn't written in English for English Canadians—it was written in French for French Canadians. All the English versions of the anthem are either translations of the original or brand-new words fitted to an existing melody. The story of Calixa Lavallée and of his anthem is a tale almost exclusively of French Canada, of the pride and politics and culture of that part of our collective identity we so often keep from view, especially those of us in the political biosphere we still charmingly, anachronistically, call "English" Canada. To so thoroughly ignore French Canada is to misunderstand Lavallée, "O Canada," and our historical reality as a nation.

In 1980, on the centenary of its first performance, the late, revered Peter Gzowski and I talked about the anthem on CBC's *Morningside*. Peter, proud Canadian that he was, noted how ironic it was that "O Canada" was premiered on St. Jean Baptiste Day, the national holiday of Quebec, the single day of the year most associated with Quebec nationalism. Of course, there was no irony in that date at all. Or actually the irony was greater than he realized. "O Canada" was premiered on St. Jean Baptiste Day because it was commissioned by the Saint-Jean-Baptiste Society in 1880 to be a "Chant national,"as it was then titled—a national anthem, exclusively for French Canada. The original Canada of "O Canada" ended at the Quebec border.

That today we can use the same song for a pan-Canadian national hymn is based on a linguistic sleight of hand, that the same word, *Canada*—Indigenous in origin, of course—is used by French Canada to refer to its ancient Laurentian homeland and by the rest of us to refer to the sea-to-sea Dominion we started to knit together in 1867. In effect, we have managed a bit of political and cultural alchemy with "O Canada," turning an anthem for part of us into one for us all. We have appropriated the song to serve a wider purpose, and expanded the "terre de nos aïeux" (land of our ancestors) of the French original into "our home and native land," something larger, more inclusive. In effect, two visions of the country exist within the bosom of a single song.

The reason we've been able to do that is because Calixa Lavallée, this unique French Canadian composer, wove into the music of "O Canada" a vitality and spirit that speaks clearly and majestically on its own—without words, or even with sets of different words. In the mysterious way that music works, there is something in the melody and rhythm and harmony and inner being of "O Canada" that taps into the psyche of a nation and displays it in sound. It is no easy feat, and is rarely done. Most anthems borrow already-existing music composed for some other purpose altogether.

But not "O Canada." "O Canada" was a deliberate and successful attempt at a *chant national* by a single individual. An individual who, whether he knew it or not, deposited a lifetime of experiences into the few bars of a song he composed in only a few weeks in 1880—his own experiences, but also those of his culture and his nation. To understand "O Canada" is to know the rollicking, tempestuous, conflicted, uniquely Canadian, uniquely French Canadian story of its composer. A story, completely unexpected and dramatic, of one of the great Canadian lives—great, but virtually unknown, even in today's Quebec. Repatriated in the 1930s from Boston, where it was originally located, today Lavallée's grave, in the Notre-Dame-des-Neiges Cemetery atop Mount Royal in Montreal, calmly looks over the city that treated him with a frustrating mixture of adulation and indifference when he was alive.

This is Calixa Lavallée's story—as interesting as any in Canadian history. It is uniquely his, but it also stands for all the contradictions and confusions of Canadian history and identity as our country began to coalesce in the last half of the nineteenth century. To understand "O Canada," and the man who wrote it, is to return to the Canada of that period, a nation in utero, bringing together ancient racial hatreds and novel political possibilities as culture faced culture, religion faced religion, economy faced economy. It was a time before the country's history had assumed the boring, neat, tidy chronology that we learned in school; when, instead, its citizens were gripped with political confusion and excitement—a time when various forces of change on the North American continent were bumping and banging wantonly into each other. A waning British colonialism; an America reeling from and weakened by its Civil War; a Canada both fearful and excited for its future; a Quebec confused and torn by its past, its future, and its agonized present—this was the backdrop to the life of Calixa Lavallée.

When you add to that whirlpool of political and cultural turbulence an artist of superior talent with a personality addicted to adventure, a mind clear and concise, and a temperament both calculating and wild, you have a first-rate tale—the story of a man who, among other things, sat down at his piano in Quebec City in the spring of 1880 and stood up soon thereafter with a nation's soul on a piece of paper in his hand.

ONE

A S YOU DRIVE south and east of Montreal, you leave behind the vast, yawning majesty of the St. Lawrence River. It's not hard to imagine the awe with which the original inhabitants of this land, Indigenous and European both, viewed this sprawling, powerful artery, splitting a landscape in two, beckoning with its watery promise voyages to parts unknown, a liquid nerve that fired imaginations and peoples.

Even today, the river has the power to make us stop and wonder. At this point in its concourse, 1,100 kilometres from the Gulf of St. Lawrence, it is deep and broad, almost 3,500 metres wide, overshadowing everything around it. But as you head south and then east, another river begins to insinuate itself into the landscape—the Richelieu, not as powerful or majestic as the St. Lawrence, but still active and aggressive, with so much of Quebec's history rolled into its banks and valleys.

As you turn off the highway onto the simple, rural rue Labonté, up ahead there's a slightly bent green sign that tells you you're about to enter the town of Calixa-Lavallée. The town barely contains five hundred souls today, probably not many more than when its namesake was born here in 1842. You turn off down chemin de la Beauce (known as rang de la Beauce in 1842), just a sweet little country road with the commanding steeple of a beautiful stone church dominating the landscape. In between the modern bungalows and garish pubs are some stately houses lovingly restored to their nineteenth-century glory—and then suddenly you pass the monument and plaque, the little park where the house in which Calixa Lavallée was born stood until 1949, before it was destroyed by fire. There's a beautiful iron sign on the site, so weathered now by age it can hardly be read, that informs you that the author of "O Canada" was born here, and a modern, laminated display tells the story of Calixa Lavallée, his famous composition, and his amazing life. And, unexplained, there's an ancient forge just behind the educational display, perhaps one that actually belonged to Lavallée's blacksmith father.

It was in 1836, according to the sign, that Augustin Lavallée, Calixa's father, moved to this spot between the St. Lawrence and Richelieu Rivers. Behind what would have been the house, the farms and fields are still laid out as they were four hundred years ago, in those long, straight, very French Canadian parcels of seigneurial property. No other part of Canada looks remotely like this. History here is as close as the land under your feet.

And it was this place that nurtured a sentiment which managed to find its way into a little tune, a few bars long, that continues to inspire a nation. A nation that didn't exist when Calixa Lavallée was born, but which now stretches 2,500 kilometres to the east from here, 4,600 to the west, and 2,800 to the north, but less than 100 to the south. It is here that our story must begin, in this small park in the southwest of Quebec. As much as the story of Calixa Lavallée and "O Canada" is one that belongs to the whole country, it also belongs to the province to which this little spot belongs: the province of Quebec, the province of the mind and heart that is French

Canada. The St. Lawrence that flows so placidly not far from here eventually traces out almost the entire geographic extent of the wider Dominion. But it is also the lifeblood, the main artery, that held together and still holds together a unique people with their own language and laws and customs and history and character. Calixa Lavallée travelled widely in his life and lived in many places, all more sophisticated than this one. But in many respects, he remained a child of this place, of its geography and history and lore, all his life. The French-Canadian culture to which he was an heir informed his sensibility, providing him a bulwark and an identity that he carried with him throughout his life as he travelled the continent and crossed the ocean. Lavallée's patriotism was not of an especially demonstrative sort, as we shall see. He held many conflicting opinions about his community and his culture. He lived a good part of his life in the United States. But that French Canada was his cultural base, his spiritual home, was never in any doubt. If we want to understand the man who wrote the national anthem for an entire country, we need to understand his attachment to just this part of it. It was the emotional topography and unifying ground for his life, a combination of language and custom and history within which he nestled his personal identity.

Calixa Lavallée could trace his French Canadian ancestry back seven generations to one Isaac Pasquier dit Lavallée, who arrived in Canada in 1665. Isaac was a soldier, part of a regiment that was dispatched to the royal colony of New France by King Louis XIV to help put down an Iroquois uprising. When his military mission was finished two years later, Isaac, like many of his colleagues, decided to stay in the New World, encouraged by a land grant from the royal government. In 1670, he married Élisabeth Meunier, a woman who could trace her Canadian heritage back another generation, to the 1640s, and the Lavallée family was established for good in North America. Isaac Pasquier dit Lavallée was Calixa Lavallée's great-great-great-great-great-grandfather.

For a hundred years, the Lavallées, and other families just like theirs, settled their roots into the soil around the St. Lawrence River as part of the French royal colony that had established itself there in the 1630s, and which had flourished ever since. Under the twin suns of the French monarchy and the Catholic Church, the community had arranged itself around the contending forces of the habitant, the settler, and the *coureur de bois*, the fur trader. Although the habitant created the sinews of what would eventually become French Canadian culture, with its emphasis on the home and the family, it was the fur trade that was the beating heart of the colony, the enterprise that provided it an expansive and dramatic reach across half the continent. The century and a half of French rule in Quebec was a tumultuous one, with battles between natives and settlers and between French Canada and British America dominating its life. It was a culture of heroes and martyrs, of drama and conflict, but above all it was a culture of settlement and continuity, marked out by the grand pillars of French language, French law, and the Catholic religion, but by many small pillars as well—the hundreds of thousands of acts of community and life passages a people celebrates together. The continuity of French Canada, its longevity and persistence, became one of its most important features.

And then, of course, that continuity was destroyed—thrown into disarray, or so it seemed, by the military and political events of 1759, by the Battle of the Plains of Abraham and the Treaty of Paris, by "the Conquest." All of a sudden, New France belonged to England. The French governors departed, the French soldiers were gone, the fur trade passed from French to English hands. Only the Church remained as a rock against which French Canada could stabilize itself. The Lavallées and their compatriots must have been terrified and anxious to know their fate after England assumed control of the colony in 1763. But their way of life didn't disappear. The British might have tried to assimilate the 50,000 French Canadians they inherited at the Conquest, but they didn't. The Conquest certainly changed the emotional temperature of French Canada—it still hangs over the province of Quebec like a vaguely menacing cloud. But it didn't halt the development of French-Canadian culture. If anything, it accelerated it. Falling back on their history and institutions, warmed by their language and customs, and embraced by their church, French Canadians deepened their ties to one another and to the land from which they had come. They may have, by necessity, developed a new defensiveness about their way of life—and in the years just before Calixa Lavallée's birth, they had to defend it by force of arms—but it was a vital culture into which Lavallée was born.

...

Calixa Lavallée was born here, off le rang de la Beauce, in the parish of Saint-François-Xavier-de-Verchères, on December 28, 1842, the first child of Jean-Baptiste Augustin Lavallée and Charlotte-Caroline Valentine. Augustin Lavallée had been born in the Richelieu Valley, not far from here, in 1816. He started his career by following his father into the family business—blacksmithing—and was apprenticed as a teenager.

But Augustin Lavallée wanted to be more than a simple blacksmith—he harboured a deep love and a talent for music. In his twenties, he attended a college north of Montreal for his education and there met one Joseph Casavant. Like Augustin, Casavant was also a blacksmith's son with a love of music who enjoyed tinkering with and building things. So when the college needed an organ it had imported from Europe assembled into a finished product, Casavant seemed the logical person to ask. From this simple beginning, Joseph Casavant eventually founded one of the great organ-manufacturing companies in North America, still in existence today—Casavant Frères. For a few years after their college days, Augustin Lavallée worked for Casavant, helping him construct his instruments and performing on them as well. He was Casavant's demonstration artist, in effect, showing off the new instruments once they were completed.

In his mid-twenties, however, Augustin Lavallée returned to his native Richelieu Valley, resumed his blacksmith business, and within a year had married Charlotte-Caroline Valentine. Calixa arrived soon after (he was actually baptized Calixte), the first of thirteen Lavallée children, many of whom entered the music business in one way or another: brother Charles was a fine trombonist; brother Joseph led a band; sister Cordelia was a vocalist.

Augustin stayed here, in this picturesque part of the Richelieu Valley, for six years altogether, building up his blacksmith business but also branching out into instrument making and repair. Eventually he would become the most famous violin maker in the province. His first son spent his very early years in this beautiful part of the world. However, when Calixa was four, after the birth of a second child, Augustin moved his family south to Saint-Hyacinthe, a town of three thousand, where Casavant had set up shop. Gradually, Augustin gave up blacksmithing for his second career. Music became the family business.

It was in Saint-Hyacinthe that Calixa Lavallée's talents as a musical prodigy were first noticed. He clearly loved the atmosphere of his father's shop; it was his first music school. Music was everywhere. Augustin was noted for being able to play just about any musical instrument there was—the better to repair it—and he developed a reputation as a fine bandleader as well. No surprise then that Calixa, with his innate musical ability, was equally adept on piano, violin, and cornet—he would eventually play all three professionally. Music became his playground as well as his delight. According to one story, his first public performance was following his father's band down the street in Verchères, merrily banging his cymbals with total abandon. He was three.

Augustin Lavallée was Calixa's first and, for a long time, only teacher, and it soon became clear that the young boy had something other than a normal talent for music. The stories about his early prowess may be exaggerated, but not necessarily. By one account, he was playing the organ expertly at Saint-Hyacinthe's Notre-Dame-du-Rosaire by age ten. In another, at seven or eight, he was writing down music he had heard a band play while sitting on the Verchères wharf, feet dangling in the St. Lawrence. He supposedly began composing at age nine. He was certainly playing in his father's band as a regular cornet player as a pre-teen. His ability to play several instruments and his enormous facility on them all created a reputation for this Saint-Hyacinthe kid that eventually spread outside this tiny community on the Yamaska River and reached all the way to Montreal.

Saint-Hyacinthe was a predominantly francophone community, but one English family, the Unsworths, became important in Lavallée's career. Mary Unsworth was the sister of a famous American pianist, and her son James Jr. eventually became a leading minstrel performer. Whether through them or through others, word of Calixa Lavallée's talent spread outside the community and eventually came to the attention of Léon Derome in Montreal. Derome was a butcher by day, but he was also a supporter and connoisseur of the arts, a patron and scout, a man intensely devoted to musical talent wherever he could find and support it. Derome had heard tales of this young Saint-Hyacinthe prodigy, and at one point he managed to hear young Calixa play the piano. He became a convert and immediately decided to help further the young man's musical education. His plan was to take Lavallée back to Montreal with him and try to secure professional instruction for this budding genius.

He was ultimately successful, and eventually Derome convinced Augustin Lavallée to let Calixa come to Montreal and live in the Derome household. Derome virtually adopted the young musician, providing him with spending money, involving him in family events, and, most importantly, arranging his studies with a couple of Montreal's best-known piano teachers. It was the fall of 1855. Calixa Lavallée was twelve. He said goodbye to his parents and siblings, got in Derome's carriage, and left home. He wouldn't live with his family again for eight years, with many adventures in between.

...

As Calixa Lavallée left the Richelieu Valley, he may not have known that a key moment in French-Canadian history—one that would shape him and French Canada profoundly—had occurred more or less where his carriage was travelling. It was the one time that tensions between French and English Quebecers had exploded into violence, and it happened just five years before Lavallée was born and just a few kilometres from where he lived.

Because on November 23, 1837, near the village of Saint-Denis, just fifteen kilometres south of the Lavallée home, a significant battle took place between Quebec nationalists—les Patriotes, as they styled themselves—and the British colonial forces opposing them. The battle was the beginning of the famous Rebellions of

1837 and 1838 in both Lower and Upper Canada, that have become so central to Canadian history. In Upper Canada, the little stroll that William Lyon Mackenzie and his four hundred supporters took down Yonge Street from Montgomery's Tavern in December of 1837 occasioned a skirmish of about twenty minutes' length, resulting in no casualties (although there had been deaths in other clashes in previous days). Modern Stanley Cup celebrations have created more havoc. But in Lower Canada, the violence and bloodshed associated with the Rebellions was very real, very widespread, and permanently traumatic to the consciousness of French Canada. It reverberates to this day in Quebec.

There were three battles in all in the Lower Canadian Rebellions in 1837. The Patriotes managed to prevail at that first encounter in Saint-Denis, but not before up to sixty-six combatants died in the conflict, mainly on the rebel side. Two days later, at Saint-Charles, the British successfully avenged their loss, killing another fifty Patriotes. (According to one family story, Augustin Lavallée and his father decided to join the fight at Saint-Charles on the rebel side, walking the twelve kilometres to the battlefield from their home, but arrived too late.) The final battle of the 1837 Rebellions occurred at Saint-Eustache: a decisive British victory, another 70 Patriotes killed. All in all, including more skirmishes in 1838, the Lower Canada Rebellions caused over three hundred deaths, and the wounding or capture of another sixteen hundred, mainly on the Patriote side. And it didn't end there. The British army went on a rampage of pillage, destruction, and rape in the Richelieu Valley after their final victories. No British soldiers were ever brought to justice, but twenty-nine leaders of the Rebellion were executed, with another fifty-eight exiled to Australia. (The famous song "Un Canadien errant" was written about those Australian exiles.)

No wonder the British government reacted with such alacrity in response to the 1837 and 1838 Rebellions, sending Lord Durham to Lower Canada within months of the end of hostilities with a commission to discover what had caused such fury. The Rebellion in that province had been serious and bloody.

The violence that erupted on the battlefields of the Richelieu Valley was likely inevitable, given the history of New France after the British Conquest. The British government did not, as we have noted, destroy French culture when they inherited New France. Unique among their colonial possessions, they allowed Quebec to retain its language, laws, customs, and religion. They may have done so out of diffidence, or they may have done so to provide a bulwark against American colonies already asserting their independence, but the result was that for Calixa Lavallée's ancestors, as for many other families who had made Quebec their home, their hundred-year-long history in the New World didn't end with the assumption of British rule. It changed, though, and made of the habitants an odd, reduced people, with the danger of English supremacy and control a constant threat to their culture and very being.

Eventually, French Canadians pushed back against the English domination of their province, and especially against the new commercial, grasping, rapacious values of the English merchant class that had become so powerful in Quebec. And they used political power to do so. It was the first time in French Canadian history that an inchoate feeling of nationalism was turned into something more pointed and powerfully deliberate.

The British government had granted Quebec a limited form of democracy when they split the province into Upper and Lower Canada in 1791. Part of the new political set-up was a legislative assembly, popularly elected; although it had few real powers, it became a focal point for the new French Canadian political class that emerged within the province at the beginning of the 1800s. The Parti canadien, later to be called the Parti patriote, was the chief vehicle for French Canadian political expression at this time, and under the eventual leadership of Louis-Joseph Papineau it dominated the popularly elected Assembly in the province, due to Lower Canada's enormous French Canadian population.

But the conflicts between the rural, agrarian, traditional French Canadians in the Assembly and the forward-looking, commercially minded, modern businessmen in the rest of the government inevitably meant that the political situation in Lower Canada became increasingly deadlocked and increasingly dysfunctional. Tensions ran high, and in 1834 Papineau submitted his Ninety-Two Resolutions to London as a plan to reform the institutions of democracy in Lower Canada and reaffirm the traditional French values for which the Parti patriote stood.

For three years, the Resolutions were completely ignored by the British government, and when they finally were addressed, they were all summarily dismissed. It was the last straw for Papineau and les Patriotes. The armed Rebellions, now impossible to avoid, began just a few months later.

The significance of the 1837 conflict to nationalist Quebecers was not simply that they lost the battles in the Richelieu Valley. It was the viciousness of the British response to the Rebellions which focused their attention, and provided them their lessons for the future. For the first time, it became desperately clear that there was a considerable price to be paid for daring to be a French Canadian in French Canada: some three hundred deaths, thirteen hundred imprisonments, twenty-nine executions, fifty-eight exiles. The 1837 Rebellions still reverberate in French Canada for that reason. But if anything, that oversized response made French Canadian nationalism even more intense, the determination to stay true to traditional

French values even more profound. It hardened French Canadians and forged a new defensiveness in their soul.

It was precisely in this cauldron of emotion and political controversy that Calixa Lavallée came of age. Very soon after he left home, he would undoubtedly have become aware of the events that had transpired so close to where he grew up. He may even have known about them before he left.

...

Montreal must have been completely dazzling to the twelve-year-old Calixa Lavallée when he first saw it in 1855. A burgeoning city of sixty thousand, more or less equally split between anglophones and francophones, bustling with life, it was twenty times larger than where he had come from. Each of the grand concert halls of the city could hold half the entire population of Saint-Hyacinthe. Montreal in the mid-1850s was starting to take on some of the aspects of its current urban landscape. Two of the great churches of the city, Notre-Dame and St. Patrick's, had already been built. Marketplaces were being established throughout the city. An increasing industrialization was attracting people from all over the province to the metropolis, which made it by far the largest and most important city in British North America. Montreal was just emerging from an economic downturn when Calixa Lavallée moved to Léon Derome's house, and it was beginning to recover some of its appetite for music, culture, and entertainment. There were several first-class performing facilities in the city, including Mechanics' Hall and the Theatre Royal, a 1,500-seat facility where everyone from solo classical artists to minstrel troupes to vaudeville performers could and did appear.

But in the Montreal of the 1850s, and for many decades

thereafter, entertainment and serious performance were not things the community felt it could provide itself. They needed to be imported. (Lavallée was still complaining of this trend twenty-five years later.) Touring companies regularly put Montreal on their itineraries, and over the years, the city got to see many American minstrel troupes and comedy acts, the occasional opera company working its way across the Northeast, travelling theatre companies—whoever happened to be on the road. Sometimes it was a celebrity performer, like the American pianist Louis Moreau Gottschalk or the "Swedish Nightingale," Jenny Lind, who was brought in by P.T. Barnum. In 1855, the year that Lavallée arrived in the city, Adelina Patti, destined to become one of the great opera stars of the world, gave a Montreal performance—she, too, was only twelve. Camilla Urso, another prodigy, this time on the violin, also came through town, as did the famous violinist Ole Bull. Sigismond Thalberg, a pianist who was the contemporary and rival of Franz Liszt, gave three concerts in the city in 1857. These were all surely exciting and inspiring occasions for the young Lavallée, especially the concerts of the young prodigies, who were no older than himself. However, the notion that Quebecers might be able to make their own music at a professional level was virtually unheard of at the time. In many ways, that attitude, in both French and English Canada, didn't really begin to change until the 1950s.

Lavallée's musical life in Montreal was dominated by private lessons, arranged by Léon Derome, with two of the city's most famous teachers. The first was Paul Letondal, who was impressed enough with young Lavallée's ability that he agreed to teach him for free. Letondal was a fascinating figure in mid-century Quebec. Born in France, blind from an early age, he nonetheless played both piano and cello well, was an astute businessman and a music journalist, and had been a student of famed pianist Friedrich

Kalkbrenner in Paris before he came to Canada in 1852. Lavallée seems to have studied with him for several years and admired him greatly.

Lavallée's other influence and teacher during these very early years was a unique Quebec figure, Charles Sabatier. Born to a French mother and a German father, he was a romantic, unconventional, and dashingly controversial figure in the austere new world of mid-century Quebec. A composer, a pianist, a bon vivant, a bohemian, Sabatier wrote music, played piano with great élan, gave a famous two-hour recital entirely made up of his own compositions, and was probably Lavallée's teacher around 1856 or 1857. Years later, pieces by Sabatier were still in Lavallée's piano repertoire.

As is true for many developing artistic societies, a native theatre scene appeared in Montreal before a native musical scene appeared and it's likely that Lavallée's first professional engagements were as a member of a pit orchestra providing incidental music for a theatrical production. Several French-language theatre companies began operations while Lavallée was in Montreal, and it was common for music to be heard at intermissions at these performances. So it was that on February 28, 1859, between performances of *Vildac* and *La carte à payer* by a group called Les Amateurs Canadiens, Calixa Lavallée played a piano recital at intermission. After having been in Montreal for four years, it was his solo public debut. He was sixteen.

La minerve, a leading Montreal political journal, noted the performance in its review of the evening:

We must not conclude without mentioning the first appearance on a Montreal stage of a young Canadian pianist, Mr. Lavallée of Saint-Hyacinthe; a well-deserved reputation preceded this artist to Montreal, and the different pieces that he played were greeted with thunderous applause; and, to please the avid audience, he was obliged to return to the stage many times. These successes assure him of one of the most distinguished positions among the small number of artists we possess in Canada.

The critic of *La minerve* surely did not know how accurate his predictions for Lavallée would be. But Lavallée's growing reputation, based on such reviews, won him an even more prestigious second public gig: a gala concert on June 24, 1859, organized by the famous and influential Saint-Jean-Baptiste Society to mark the end of a day of celebrations for Saint-Jean-Baptiste Day, which would eventually become Quebec's official national holiday. Among a lineup that included amateur vocalists, a quadrille band, and an orchestra, the concert began with "M. Lavallée, au Piano." In addition to being a Saint-Jean-Baptiste Day concert, it was also a fundraiser for a monument to the victims of the Rebellions of 1837 and 1838, still on Quebec's mind twenty years after the fact.

So, at just sixteen, here was Lavallée in the summer of 1859: a potentially good, if not great, classical artist, turning critical heads, with a loyal patron—an artist full of promise in a society on the brink of something great as well, or so it seemed, less than a decade before Confederation. His potential seemed unlimited.

But he had other plans, or perhaps no plans at all. All his life, as we shall see, Calixa Lavallée was driven, almost against his will, by a seemingly predestined wanderlust. It led him out of his native society, out of conventional experience, into something quite different and unexpected, even radical. He was a young man when he made his first steps in this direction, full of an innocent confidence that he could conquer any and all worlds. But he was motivated as well by a desire for change and excitement that would reappear in his life again and again. Nothing in Lavallée's life was entirely predictable.

And so, despite the promising future that seemed to be opening up in front of him, Calixa Lavallée just up and left Quebec a few short weeks after that Saint-Jean-Baptiste Day concert in 1859. He made his way down to Providence, Rhode Island, to join a group run by Charles Duprez and John Green—the New Orleans and Metropolitan Burlesque Opera Troupe and Brass Band.

Which was not a brass band, nor a burlesque opera troupe, nor from New Orleans.

Duprez and Green were minstrels. White performers who put burnt cork on their hands and faces and paraded as black entertainers across the physical and psychological terrain of the United States. They had been doing so for years, since the 1840s—taking part in perhaps the most significant cultural phenomenon in America's two-hundred-year history. Minstrelsy was important to America, forcing the new nation to encounter questions of race, class, and politics in the transgressive confines of the minstrel-show theatre. Eventually Duprez and Green, later Duprez and Benedict, would run one of the most famous minstrel troupes in U.S. history.

In the fall of 1859, Calixa Lavallée joined this fraternity, and not just for a lark. For ten years of his life, Lavallée would make his living as a minstrel. Until his mid-twenties, it was the only job he had ever had. In setting out on this path, he left behind him his home, his family, his burgeoning career, classical music, and the province of Quebec. He had run away to join a very special, complex, radical, and questionable circus. The future composer of "O Canada" had begun a tumultuous, and completely unexpected, career.

TWO

IT IS HARD TO IMAGINE. The author of "O Canada," arrayed in blackface, contorting himself into ridiculous postures, playing the cornet, violin, and piano in a mainstream, raucous, low-brow, racist minstrel show. But there he was, burnt cork and all. Mugging and dancing, mincing across the minstrel stage, for an adoring audience. And he was good at it. Calixa Lavallée eventually became a leading musician on the minstrel circuit in the United States, a highly sought-after musical director, leading the band, writing original songs, and arranging the music for a series of troupes, ending with the San Francisco Minstrels, one of the most famous of them all. Starting in 1859, just before he turned seventeen, Lavallée "blacked up" for years—first between 1859 and 1861, again for a year in 1862 and 1863, then for a third stretch lasting seven long years, between 1866 and 1873. Something about the glamour of the minstrel world, something about its excitement and freedom, something about its forbidden character seems to have exercised an enormous attraction on this young musician from out there in the Canadian hinterland.

Today, we recoil in horror at the stunningly overt racism of the minstrel show, that spectacle where white entertainers disguised themselves as "Ethiopian delineators," as they called themselves, to mimic, degrade, and humiliate black Americans. All for the delight of white audiences throughout the United States, in both North and South. And in Canada as well—the minstrel circuit had many regular stops north of the border. Today, we can't quite believe or accept the baldness of the racial hostility of minstrelsy and so we hastily sidestep it, consign it to the curiosity shop of North American popular culture along with marathon dancing and flagpole sitting, despite its decidedly more racial charge. We don't want to look at its reality directly or clearly, and prefer to think it was just one of those unaccountable things that all societies find in their histories, dark anachronisms thankfully long buried in a culture's past. That a Canadian—the author of our national anthem, no less—was part of this phenomenon, we register as fascinating but incidental.

However, decades of recent scholarship into minstrelsy have made us rethink our interpretation of the form and have forced us to recognize that minstrelsy was a tremendously important brand of American culture, beyond and despite its racism. Minstrelsy was racist, no doubt, but it was also nineteenth-century America's TV, movies, pop music, and Broadway all rolled into one, immensely popular and significant. It was a sharp but effective tool with which an emerging industrial working-class population could try to pry open an understanding of itself in its new urban, alienated form of life. It was a cultural vehicle by which high and low forms of art were brought together and mediated, where satire was used to deflate the pompous, where pop music emerged as a political and cultural expression of American values, and where an authentic American cultural vernacular began to be created. Even the racism of minstrelsy turns out to be much more complex than imagined, with hatred and scorn of the black man intermixed with envy, sexual jealousy, admiration, and identification. Minstrelsy was one of the most complex social phenomena of North American history. Its widespread appeal helped it not only tap into but also form the cultural, social, and psychological essence of America in the decades just before and after the Civil War. As much as any other institution of its time, if not more so, it was central to the development of an American character and an American ethos. And at its core, at the heart of its appeal, was the fact that it was deeply subversive.

Now, exactly how much of this overarching cultural analysis would have dawned on a sixteen-year-old Calixa Lavallée in 1859 is hard to know. (It was the move to the minstrel troupe that got the young Calixte to change his name to Calixa.) More likely, Lavallée would have just been taken up with the glamour, excitement, and sheer fun of his new career. We have to speculate, because Lavallée in his later life went to great pains to suppress and obscure his minstrel past, never speaking about it, even going so far as to concoct imaginary tales of musical journeys around the world to cover off the ten years of minstrelsy in his biography. Exactly how Lavallée ended up in a minstrel show is also unknown. Several companies made regular stops in Montreal, so he would have known how the shows worked, and he might even have approached one of them to see if he could join. More likely, it was his friendship with James Unsworth, a former Saint-Hyacinthe neighbour and a leading minstrel performer, that led him into the blackface world. But in an odd way, it actually seems natural, if unconventional, for Lavallée to have become a minstrel. Here's a kid brimming with talent, with virtually nowhere to ply his trade in the stultifying French Canadian society of his day. Rather than give a piano recital or two every few months for eighty people and a few dollars, here was a well-paying, exciting job in the glamorous world of the theatre, where you played to hundreds if not thousands every night to great acclaim. Why not become a minstrel? It probably was not that difficult a decision for Lavallée to make. And yet, as much of a lark as it may have seemed at the time, Lavallée's career in minstrelsy eventually taught him some very important lessons. It showed him the power of music to rouse a people and define a culture. It would become clear many years later that these lessons had not been lost on him.

Lavallée began his minstrel career with the extravagantly named New Orleans and Metropolitan Burlesque Opera Troupe and Brass Band better known as the New Orleans Minstrels. Despite their name, the New Orleans Minstrels were based in Providence, Rhode Island, founded by one of the great impresarios of the American minstrel theatre, Charles Duprez. Aside from a few episodes with other outfits, Lavallée spent his entire minstrel career in Duprez shows. Duprez liked to tell people that he was born in France and emigrated to Quebec before he set up business in the U.S. His obituary—likely more accurate—states that he was born in Lowell, Massachusetts, and worked his way into the business from there. Either way, Duprez drew upon his French-sounding name and linked it to the French heritage of New Orleans to make his troupe seem more authentically southern. Perhaps that was why he was initially attracted to French Canadian musicians like Calixa Lavallée for his band—their names helped propagate the myth that he was leading a Louisiana-based company.

But there was nothing authentic about Duprez's outfit, or about minstrelsy itself. This is one of minstrelsy's great ironies. Despite all the hype about its connection to and depiction of southern plantation life, minstrelsy was not a southern phenomenon at all, but a northern one. Nor was it a rural phenomenon, but an urban one. Its intended audience was not a generous sampling of southern grandees, but instead a raucous, disaffected, male, white working-class mob—young, rootless, and restless—assembled in places like New

York, Philadelphia, and Buffalo. Set in the romanticized South of the happy plantation family and the contented "darky," the minstrel show was a thoroughgoing appropriation of voice, not just of black America but of southern America as well. All the great minstrel performers were from working-class origins in northern cities. And, of course, all of them were white. Their connection to the rural South they so lovingly depicted in their shows was nil.

Nonetheless, these white, northern, working-class performers of minstrelsy managed to write and perform their South remarkably effectively. Classic southern anthems like "Dixie" and "Old Folks at Home" were not written by southerners, nor did they originate in the South at all. Both first saw the light of day in northern minstrel shows, written by northern composers, performed by northern working-class men in blackface. Ohio-born Dan Emmett, who wrote "Dixie" for a Bryant's Minstrels show, sang it every night of his life from 1859, when he first wrote the tune, until 1868—except, of course, during the Civil War, when he didn't dare, as the Confederacy had taken it as their unofficial national anthem. "Marching Through Georgia" was first introduced in a minstrel show, as was "Tenting on the Old Campground," a sentimental hit well into the 1890s. The history of these songs, so unexpected, is merely one demonstration of the complex, disorienting power of minstrelsy. Songs written to mimic a southern way of life by northern performers—appropriating a voice—were later re-appropriated by that same southern culture and became authentic, deeply held expressions of that culture.

Minstrelsy in America had its origins in blackface entertainment, the practice of white people disguising themselves to pass as black. Blackface has a complicated background in the folk culture of the United States, as it does in many other countries. The need to mimic and perform another culture by dressing in its clothes and reproducing its mannerisms is widespread. Blackface folk celebrations in America can be traced as far back as the 1600s. However, it was in the 1830s and 1840s that the blackface performer emerged as an enduring feature of the American entertainment scene, before the minstrel show itself was invented. In the early days of blackface entertainment, the transgressive nature of these acts was most obvious, their thrilling perversity most prominent. That was the secret of their success, even as that success was unexpected.

In 1828, Thomas Dartmouth Rice, a white Irish actor from the Lower East Side, introduced a blackface character into his act, supposedly developed by watching black men on New York's docks. This was Jim Crow, the Negro bumpkin with a sharp, boastful, yet magnetic personality. The song, dance moves, and persona that Rice invented for "Jump Jim Crow," a tune he sang tens of thousands of times over two decades, became not just one of the most successful stage acts in American entertainment history but one of the defining symbols of all American life, well beyond the stage. When the post-Confederate South decided to turn its back on Reconstruction after the Civil War and re-codify its racist policies towards its black population, the laws used to do so were called Jim Crow laws, the character remaining a potent symbol of racial oppression and intolerance. We still use the expression today.

Jim Crow touched something extremely powerful in the mind and psyche of early nineteenth-century white America: the complex psychology surrounding the racial Other. Jim Crow allowed white audiences to contain and emasculate the figure of the black male, equally feared and admired, in this purposeful theft of his persona, his being. What was feared to be looked on directly in the world could now be viewed in psychological safety in the theatre because it was filtered through a white performer, alternately copying and mocking the black man. The power of the appeal of blackface surprised even "Daddy" Rice, who eventually dropped all his other characterizations (he was an accomplished actor) to concentrate on this one creation, his alter ego, Jim Crow.

The success of Jim Crow inevitably created imitators, and Rice's creation was soon followed by another caricature from a second white entertainer. George Washington Dixon's Zip Coon embodied the other enduring black stereotype in the white American imagination: the urban dandy. Unlike Jim Crow's innocent boyishness, Zip Coon was from thes start a figure of sexual menace and allure. His "Long-Tail Blue," the euphemistic black penis, a Jungian symbol of fear and attraction for white America, was never far from the psychic surface of Dixon's character. Of course, this was the point of these images: to allow audiences to play with the psychological dynamite of the forbidden and the fearsome within the safety of the theatre, and to keep just under control the dynamic power of the sexual intersection of black and white America.

The transgressive appeal of Jim Crow and Zip Coon, originally presented as single acts, gave some blackface performers the idea to create entire evening-length variety shows based on blackface traditions and the many complex and free-floating valences of their implications. Thus was born the minstrel show proper, first created by four entertainers led by Dan Emmett, the "Dixie" composer, calling themselves the Virginia Minstrels (Emmett, remember, was from Ohio). In 1843, the Virginia Minstrels presented the first complete show based on blackface entertainment, at the Bowery Amphitheatre in New York. From that point on, the minstrel show was the most significant form of popular entertainment in America—it would remain so for the next sixty years, with an influence on popular culture that lasted well into the twentieth century. There are film performances of white entertainers in blackface into the 1930s (Fred Astaire "blacked up" in a tribute to famed dancer Bill Robinson in 1936's *Swing Time*), and well into the 1960s minstrel shows were part of high school graduation entertainment in the south (Elvis appeared in one during his time at Humes High in Memphis).

Forgotten now, minstrelsy was for many years a powerful force in the United States. It was racist at its core, but its branches bore significant cultural fruit—minstrelsy provides a great deal of the hidden foundation, still, of American popular song, drama, and entertainment.

. . .

As minstrel shows gained in popularity in the 1840s and 1850s, some troupes found permanent theatres for themselves in major centres like New York, Philadelphia, and Boston. But the minstrel show also became one of America's most significant touring enterprises, with dozens of troupes travelling throughout the country to big cities and small towns, presenting one show, or a week's worth, at a time, parading down one Main Street after another, bringing urban, big-city culture to America's heartland.

Duprez and Green's New Orleans Minstrels were one of the great touring ensembles in America. Starting from their base in Providence, Rhode Island, where Duprez lived, they would begin each year's momentous tour in the Northeast and generally make their way south, spending part of the winter months in New Orleans itself. In the spring, they would head north again, ending up back in Providence to rest in July and August before starting the same trek in the fall. Charles Duprez had started his performing career in 1852, but Duprez and Green were just in their second year of operation when Calixa Lavallée joined the troupe in the fall of 1859. He began his association with the group as a simple musician—albeit one who could play cornet, piano, and violin—but eventually became leader of the band itself. He would be in blackface for the performances, sometimes appearing on stage, sometimes in the pit; sometimes performing solo numbers, sometimes accompanying the many songs scattered throughout the show (having written some of them himself). He was one of perhaps seven musicians employed by the company.

The young kid from Saint-Hyacinthe, Quebec, now found himself bouncing in stagecoaches, riding on steamers, and travelling in the luxury of train cars as he made his way, starting in the fall of 1859, up through Maine, then down through Vermont and New Hampshire. After that, gigs in Syracuse, Buffalo, Cleveland, Cincinnati, Lexington, Nashville, Memphis, and Vicksburg before settling in to New Orleans for a month or so, in January of 1860. And then back north, through Montgomery, Savannah, Atlanta, Columbia, Charleston, Wilmington, Norfolk, Richmond, Washington, Baltimore, Philadelphia, and New York, among others. Lavallée saw more of America in a year than most Americans saw in a lifetime. In bigger locales, the New Orleans Minstrels might stay for as much as a week if the box office receipts stayed strong. In other places, one night or two would suffice. Then it was back to the wagons or the train or the steamer, on the road again. To the next town, the next small city.

When the troupe got to where they were going, depending on the size of the place, Lavallée might be performing in an opera house, a grand theatre, a plain room, or a local tavern. More often than not, the New Orleans Minstrels played in large venues otherwise devoted to legitimate theatre and opera. The venues themselves were divided into very strict seating sections, based largely on class. The ground floor was made up primarily of working-class men. For them, the show was a way to blow off steam and have some fun. These were the young men from whom the minstrel performers themselves were drawn—the men for whom blackface was first invented in America, and for whom, in taverns and bars and seedy establishments on waterfronts throughout the United States, it had first been performed.

In the first balcony, safely squirrelled away from the ground-floor mayhem where enraged patrons sometimes threw vegetables and worse at the performers, was a middle-class family audience. As the minstrel show developed and moved further away from its subversive, underclass origins, it began to actively cultivate this middle-class audience by selling itself to America as family entertainment. Over time, these "respectable" spectators, men with wives in tow, became more and more important to minstrelsy's economic health. What began as subversion ended up as mainstream conventionality.

The third level of minstrel audience—way up in the second balcony—was made up of prostitutes and hustlers, the true underclass, which had always been attracted to the theatre and was especially attracted to minstrelsy. Most of the theatres in the main cities of the United States were actually situated in the parts of town most frequented by this underclass—the Bowery in New York, for example. And the colourful inhabitants of these areas were always a prime potential audience for the minstrel show. Then—as now, to some extent—the theatre was considered a magnet for the least desirable members of society.

It was one of the great strengths of minstrelsy that it appealed to all three kinds of these urban Americans. It managed to forge a common cultural language with which all Americans could converse, allowing them to define themselves as part of a single country with a shared cultural life. "High" culture in North America never performs this function. It's been the "low" culture of vaudeville, of radio, of the movies, of television that has created a common cultural language in the United States. Minstrelsy was the start of all of it, showing up in the United States just as an urban, industrial America was beginning to emerge. Though it appealed to all, minstrelsy especially helped the young men of this new America to find their place in a complex world by confusing boundaries of race, class, and sexuality. It played at the margins of society and was actually the first "politically incorrect" form of entertainment. It thus helped reduce the dissonance of national conflicts by working both sides of any issue. When even the greatest discontinuities in America needed resolution, minstrelsy was there. Author Dale Cockrell writes, "When slavery required a national dialogue, blackface minstrelsy might have been one of the most effective of all the forms it took, for it was . . . implicitly paradoxical and dynamic."

Minstrelsy was also a lubricant for a new class in America, helping the urban proletariat accommodate more easily to their new, confusing lives by presenting spectacles of degradation of the Other, both high and low. Minstrelsy targeted politicians, lawyers, and women's rights activists as often as it did black Americans. It was far more than just a form of racist pandering. That's why the shows were as popular in Canada—where, one assumes, racial themes were somewhat less visceral—as they were in the United States. Canada knew racism, certainly, and had even known slavery. But the minstrel show's appeal north of the border had less to do with its evocations of a bucolic, racist southern lifestyle than it did with its social satire. That was true in America as well.

Exactly what Calixa Lavallée thought of this world is very hard to fathom. We do know that he scrubbed his official biography clean of all traces of his minstrel past and never spoke of this part of his life. Nonetheless, it is possible to see how central Lavallée's

working experience as a minstrel musician was to his later professional success and his overall musical personality. He turned out to
be a very serious man and musician when he finally became who
he was destined to be, so it's hard to imagine that he had no
thoughts whatsoever about the scenes he had witnessed in his minstrel career, both offstage and on. It may have been an exciting
experience for him when he began, but it surely must have started
to wear on him as he got older. There is more than a little evidence
that this was the case. It was too demanding a job for Lavallée to
just coast through it. It cannot but have affected him.

But on a strictly practical level, minstrelsy taught a young
Calixa Lavallée many valuable lessons. The first of these was how
to work, and how to work to deadline. On any given day, Lavallée
might be writing a new song, a romantic ballad or a stirring martial number, for one of the troupe's several vocalists. He might be
sketching out the musical interludes needed for one of the many
satirical and topical skits the troupe would present, which changed
all the time. And, most importantly for his later musical career,
Lavallée would be responsible for arranging the music for the
extremely elaborate opera parodies—takeoffs of the wildly popular Italian operas of the time—that inevitably formed the final act
of a minstrel show. He did all this on top of rehearsing the band
every day, adding new material, keeping the old material sharp,
and performing during the evening's show. Day in and day out.

But beyond his musical activities, so valuable for a young prac-
titioner, it's impossible that Lavallée would not have observed the
cultural importance of the shows he presented nightly. He would
have seen the power of a song attuned to the sensibility of a nation,
whether it was Dan Emmett's "Dixie" or his own "Flag of Green."
He would have understood the fluid boundary between serious
and popular art, with opera scores providing the foundation for a

great deal of the minstrel repertoire. He would have witnessed the power of music not only to entertain but also to help define an audience, a community, and a nation. All of these could be brought to bear, and were, on his own musical activities once he left the minstrel world, even as it regards the composition of "O Canada" itself. "O Canada" is not a minstrel song, but without the minstrel traditions—musical and otherwise—which Lavallée observed every night, "O Canada" certainly would have been written differently: less directly, less emotionally.

...

The minstrel show had more or less cemented itself into a fixed format by the time Lavallée joined the scene in the fall of 1859. It was presented in three parts, one following another in an order which eventually became routine. Lavallée, as bandleader, would be integral to each. The show would begin with an extravagant opening musical number, bringing all the performers on stage, in blackface, singing and dancing in grand affected style. After the raucous opening, the performers would array themselves in a semicircle, in the middle of which sat the Interlocutor, a man wearing gentleman's clothing in contrast to the outlandish outfits of the other performers. His was the only visible white face on stage, a clear reference to the southern slave owner. At the command of "Gentlemen, be seated," the rest of the minstrel performers, with their painted black faces, would sit obediently and wait until they were spoken to. Then the Interlocutor would engage in a series of puns and jokes with the two performers sitting at the end of the semicircle—the "endmen," called Tambo and Bones, their names based on the instruments they originally played. The performers who played Tambo and Bones were two of the stars of the troupe, and this opening sequence was basically a comedy routine meant to open the show on a high note, based on jokes and wordplay which survived well into the vaudeville era of the early twentieth century, and even to early stand-up comedy.

After the comic opening, a series of musical numbers—mostly Irish-style ballads with plantation themes—would follow. The lead tenor in any minstrel show was an extremely important member of the troupe, and the songs performed at this point in the show might be original—Lavallée wrote many of these for Duprez—or they might be tunes made famous by other composers. The minstrel show began the tradition of popular song in America. Songs like those that Stephen Foster wrote for Edwin Christy's Minstrels (Foster was born in Philadelphia and raised in Cincinnati) are still in the *Great American Songbook*—"Camptown Races," "Oh! Susanna," "Jeanie with the Light Brown Hair," "Old Folks at Home." Lavallée, in his position as leader of the band and chief composer for Duprez, learned first-hand how to craft an engaging, powerful melody.

After these musical numbers, another of the featured performers, still—always—in blackface, would approach centre stage and give a "stump speech," a satiric, dialect-filled rant on a social topic of the day. Despite the fact that the stump speech was always delivered in a broken-English, "black" form of speaking, it was more satire than racial parody. Political satire was a central part of the minstrel show; in some ways, it was its most significant component. Blackface became an enabling medium, a disguise that allowed white performers, paradoxically, to present themselves with greater honesty. Without question, the minstrel stump speech was the precursor to the political humour of a Will Rogers or a Mort Sahl or a Chris Rock in America. Even a Mark Twain.

After the stump speech, part one would come to a rousing close with another ensemble musical number, generally a topical song written especially for the show, called a "walk-around." It was for the close of Act One of a Bryant's Minstrels show that "Dixie" was written.

Parts two and three of the show were generally less regimented than the opening. Act Two was a combination of speeches, skits, songs—some sentimental, some comic—and straight dramatic scenes, with a big Act Two finale involving the whole company. Act Three was the most extravagant portion of the entertainment. It presented a show within a show, an hour-long full performance, often a comic version of an immensely popular opera of the day.

This was undoubtedly the key portion of the show for Calixa Lavallée, a man with ambitions in the classical world as well as in the minstrel world, a composer who would eventually write two operas of his own. The musical director of the minstrel show would be expected to rework the music of famous contemporary operas by the greatest composers of the time, people like Verdi and Rossini and Bellini, for elaborate burlesques and operatic take-offs which would provide the exciting finale to the evening. These burlesques faithfully retained the music of the original European artworks, but the plots were replaced with comic, often ridiculous, contemporary stories set in the South.

Opera was positioned in a unique cultural space in the nineteenth century, very different from today. It was a serious art with pop music appeal—perhaps the only art form that straddled class lines in America, being equally popular as "high" and "low" culture. While an emerging middle class preferred to sample their opera in palatial new opera houses, most Americans first heard opera in the raucous confines of the minstrel show. These classical music parodies may have been one of the most subversive things about the entire minstrel experience. To take a famous opera with its music intact, more or less, and turn it into a plantation farce, done up in blackface and drag, allowed minstrelsy to roam widely and potently to explore both racial and class prejudice. Opera was central to the whole ambiguous, multi-faceted world of the minstrel stage. And it was critical for Calixa Lavallée's development as a musician. Through these burlesques, Lavallée not only learned how to mimic European opera, but he actually learned the original scores themselves, the better to parody them. It was a free music school for him. As we shall see, Lavallée migrated to companies where these opera burlesques were most prominent.

The minstrel show played with the ambiguities and discontinuities of race in the safe confines of the theatre, but as the young Calixa Lavallée finished his first season with Duprez and Green in the summer of 1860 and prepared for his second, it was hard to ignore the warnings and terrible rumblings of a nation preparing to play them out in real life. As Duprez and Green's New Orleans Minstrels made their way through the country in the winter of 1860 and the spring of 1861, they were unintended witnesses of history. Lavallée and Duprez were in Indiana on November 6, 1860, when Abraham Lincoln was elected president of the United States. They had travelled south, as was usual in the winter months, and were in Louisiana when South Carolina seceded from the Union on December 20, six weeks later. Three weeks after that, Mississippi, Florida, and Alabama followed suit. Duprez and Lavallée were performing in Atlanta on the very evening Georgia seceded—January 19, 1861. That evening's performance turned out to be one of Duprez's biggest successes, as the show provided a distraction for the populace, who, according to one Atlanta newspaper, "would otherwise have shortly been in a state of stark madness from political super-excitement."

From Atlanta, the troupe headed north, and they were in

Washington just two days before Lincoln's inauguration on March 4. By this time, Jefferson Davis had already been elected president of the Confederacy. The show was in New York State when the first shots of the Civil War were fired at Fort Sumter in April. At first Duprez hoped to continue business as usual even after the war had started, but he eventually decided it was expedient to stay in the North. The troupe ended their season in Providence with a special Fourth of July show. Their plan was to "rusticate" during the summer and begin touring again in the fall, in Canada and the West Indies if necessary. Many observers actually felt the war would be over long before then.

But Calixa Lavallée had other plans, and when the fall of 1861 rolled around and Duprez and Green geared up for another season on the road, Lavallée was not with them.

He was in uniform.

On September 17, 1861, he had appeared at the Union recruiting office in Providence to enlist in the Fourth Rhode Island Volunteers as a Bandsman, First Class. He was no longer the leader of a minstrel band. He was now a member of the Federal army of the United States of America.

THREE

CALIXA LAVALLÉE'S ENTRY INTO the Union army (he was Calixa Levalley to his new comrades) may have just been another example of the wanderlust that had led him to leave home and join a minstrel troupe a couple of years earlier. Something of a lark, a new adventure for this eternally restless soul. He had traded in his minstrel costume for another uniform, and was now outfitted in the blue cap and natty jacket of the Union soldier. He wasn't alone. Behind him were thousands of other Canadians arrayed in exactly the same uniform, who had also signed up for the Union cause.

It is estimated that as many as fifty thousand Canadians, mostly French Canadians, went to fight in the U.S. Civil War—an extraordinarily high number given the population of Lower Canada. Viewed from the outside, they seemed to be citizens of one country inexplicably willing to sign on to give their lives for the defence of another. Many of these young men had lived their entire lives in Quebec, yet they left their homes, ventured south, and signed on to fight in the conflict. Canadians enlisted in five hundred different Union regiments, as well as forty-six Confederate units. They fought in virtually every major battle and every theatre of the war. It is one of the least-known facts of Canadian political life: Canadians in vast numbers fought in the Civil War.

We have to remember two things that help make sense of this staggering statistic. The first is that the men who fought in the war were not citizens of one nation fighting for another. Canada was not yet a country when the United States blew up in sectarian, regional, and moral conflict in 1861. In fact, as we shall see, it was the war itself that was a major contributing factor to the drive towards Canadian Confederation. North American British colonists tended to think of their specific colony before they thought of any overriding nation in the late 1850s and early 1860s. Their loyalties were much more specific.

And for Quebecers, or citizens of Canada East as it was called at the time, this phenomenon was intensified by a cross-border, transnational cultural affinity: French Canadians in Canada felt a deep common bond with French Canadians living in New England— in Maine, Vermont, New Hampshire, Massachusetts. French Canadians had been emigrating south for about twenty years when the war broke out, and about 150,000 of them, a tenth the population of the province, formed sizable communities in places like Fall River and Lowell, Massachusetts, and Manchester, New Hampshire. Eventually, between 1840 and 1930, a million Quebecers relocated south, mainly to work in the mill towns of New England. The result was *"La Grande hémorragie"*—the Great Hemorrhage. The expression says it all.

The enormous number of French Canadians in U.S. border states meant that French America was like a mirror image of French Canada for Quebecers. Quebecers saw themselves when they looked into their Franco-American cousins' eyes; the borders separating the two communities were relatively unimportant. Consequently, French Canadians felt themselves implicated in the conflict in which their Franco-American cousins were embroiled. If a Southern victory might have destroyed or weakened French culture in the Northern states, it was worth fighting the Confederacy to ensure that didn't happen.

The closeness of the two francophone communities in North America had political as well as emotional and cultural implications. The notion of annexation, the idea that Quebec would be better off joining the United States than Canada, had a long and powerful life in the nineteenth century. Many of the leaders of the 1837 Rebellions, including Louis-Joseph Papineau, favoured this solution to Quebec's ongoing political problem. It was an option that popped up repeatedly in Quebec in the debates around Confederation. Lavallée seems to have supported this notion all his life. The idea was that a francophone Quebec might find a more sympathetic home in a country that had already welcomed so many of its citizens than it would in a confederated Canada that welcomed none. Annexation surely would have been disastrous for French Canadians, who would have been swamped long ago by the forces of American cultural myopia, but that was not easy to see in the mid-nineteenth century.

Lavallée clearly was influenced by the threat to Franco-American culture that the war represented. He may well have joined the Union forces in the Civil War even if he were still living in Montreal. As it was, however, he was already in the United States when the war broke out, which may have been a motivating factor in his decision to enlist. Lavallée could have stayed with Duprez and Green as they made their planned trip to the Maritimes and Newfoundland in the fall of 1861, but moving so far from the action was not in his character. And he didn't need Duprez to keep playing. As a bandsman in the Union army, he would get to play every day, and would be spared, he might have thought, the horrors of the lot of the enlisted soldier. And the band that he joined, of the Fourth Rhode Island Regiment, was an excellent twenty-four-piece ensemble led by Joe Greene, one of the most famous bandleaders in pre-war America. (Lavallée would end up being his assistant bandleader.) Bandsmen were also well paid by Civil War standards, thirty-four dollars a month—hardly a fortune, but more than three times the pay of a regular enlisted soldier.

But when all is said and done, the eighteen-year-old Calixa Lavallée probably became a bandsman in the Fourth Rhode Island Volunteers for the sheer excitement of it. It was consistent with his character. Lavallée didn't need wartime fever to catch the spirit of adventure and daring that the war represented. So whether he gave it much thought or none at all, Lavallée signed up on September 17, 1861, to join the band of the Fourth Rhode Island Regiment. His cousin George had signed up the day before. Calixa Lavallée was going to war.

...

Upon his enlistment, Lavallée ended up at Camp Greene, a make-shift army camp just outside Warwick that was the rallying point for the thousands of young Rhode Islanders who were joining up in the fall of 1861. It was the beginning of his extraordinary career in the Union army, which would see him take part in some of the major battles of the war. But Lavallée wasn't in the army to fight those battles, necessarily; he was there to provide musical entertainment and comfort for the troops who were.

And just as Calixa Lavallée had managed to insert himself right in the middle of the action in popular entertainment before the war, he did the same with his band activities during the war. Music was probably more important in the Civil War than it has been in any other conflict before or since. Bands provided the Civil War soldier a taste of pleasure, a taste of comfort, a taste of reason, a hint that there was another world waiting for him when the nightmares of wartime finally ended. Music offered entertainment and morale-building inspiration for those who found themselves stuck in what became a seemingly unending campaign of unimaginable horror alternated with stupefying boredom. "Music was the one home privilege we were allowed to bring with us to the war," said one Southern recruit, in a simple expression of both the deprivations of conflict and the consolations of art. The more horrible the experience of war, the more powerful the balm music provided in response. And the Civil War was horrible almost beyond reason. Music became essential for the mental health of the entire fighting nation.

Civil War musicians were essentially non-combatants. A bandsman held a musical instrument in his hands, not a musket. But bandsmen were still soldiers. They travelled with their regiment and suffered all the same indignities—lack of sleep, infestations of lice, poor weather and worse food, or no food at all—that their comrades endured. And bandsmen had duties assigned to them during battles as well—they weren't spared the battlefield by any means. Especially during the early days of the war, before medical services became properly organized to deal with the staggering and unexpected number of casualties of the conflict, bandsmen put down their instruments once the fighting started and carried out medical duties. They assisted the surgeons attending the wounded in rude operating theatres just behind the lines of battle, or acted as stretcher-bearers, recovering fallen soldiers on the field for transport to the various makeshift hospitals littering every Civil War battlefield. These hospitals, temporary loci of trauma, fear, and sometimes relief, were horribly brutal affairs by modern standards, as medical techniques were remarkably backward in mid-nineteenth-century America. Attending upon a physician applying rudimentary medical procedures in emergency conditions, or risking your life trying to recover a wounded soldier, could be as traumatic and dangerous as doing the fighting yourself. Bandsmen were still subject to the privations and horrors of the war.

But the significance of music in the conduct of the war is clear by sheer numbers alone. Although we have better statistics for the North, the tale the War Office's numbers tell probably reflects Southern reality as well. By December of 1861, just three months after Lavallée joined the Fourth Rhode Island Regiment, there were 618 different bands active in the Union army—28,000 musicians in all. That number amounted to more than one in forty members of the army—a staggering 2.5 per cent of the total Union forces. Eventually, the Union army called a halt to recruitment of new band members and mustered out thousands of existing bandsmen—it was just costing them too much money (by one estimate five million dollars annually).

The reason there were so many bands on both the Union and Confederate sides was that music worked so well to satisfy military objectives. In the first place, bands were great recruiting tools, and in a war where more than two and a half million soldiers were needed between the two sides, recruitment was a constant challenge. But what young man could resist the martial might of a tight twenty-four-piece band, brass instruments gleaming, outdoing the noonday sun, marching up Main Street in glorious array? Not many. As a recruiting tool alone, regimental bands were worth the price, or so many commanders thought.

But that was just the beginning. During the long periods between battles, or while the army was on the road, bands provided desperately needed entertainment and relaxation for soldiers in camp and on the march. Bands serenaded officers when they gathered for social occasions; they played concerts for the enlisted men; they even performed for civilians who visited the camps. They gave an immensely important morale boost to the troops facing the unknown of the next day's privations, or boredom, or terror.

And perhaps the bandsmen's most important duties occurred when an engagement was near, and the natural fear of battle rose up most powerfully in the minds and hearts of the soldiers on both sides. The music the bands would play on these occasions was not at all what you might expect. For every "Dixie" and "Battle Hymn of the Republic" the musicians would blare out, there would just as often be a paraphrase from an opera by Bellini or Verdi, or a sentimental pop song. Ballads, quicksteps on Bellini's "Casta diva," arias from *I puritani*, waltzes, galops, and polkas—the Civil War bands played them all. As well, thousands of songs on war themes were published between 1861 and 1865, and these also made their way into the bandsman's playbook. Lavallée wrote several himself when he was still with Duprez and Green, just before he enlisted. The first, "Col. Ellsworth Gallopade," celebrated the heroism of an early Union soldier. Many of the songs from the Civil War have entered the traditional repertoire and have stayed there: "John Brown's Body," adapted as "The Battle Hymn of the Republic"; "Maryland, My Maryland," which still precedes each running of the Preakness Stakes; "When Johnny Comes Marching Home Again"; and a song for the dead used by both sides, written after the Seven Days Battles in 1862—"Taps." And, of course, there was "Dixie," originally a minstrel song, popular in both North and South, which became the unofficial anthem of the Confederacy. As Robert E. Lee himself said, justifying the number of bands under his command, "I don't think we could have an army without music."

Calixa Lavallée was right in the middle of this essential enterprise. Lavallée more than likely played the saxhorn in the Fourth Rhode Island band, a brass instrument developed by Adolphe Sax, inventor of the saxophone. The saxhorn looked like a regular trumpet except that the bell from which the sound emanated was not in front of the musician, as it is with the modern trumpet, but curved around the player's shoulder so that it faced backwards. Which only makes sense—marching bands strode in front of their regiments, not behind them. The saxhorns made sure that the soldiers marching behind the band could hear them perfectly.

It's also quite possible that Lavallée, a very talented musician, was occasionally pressed into service as a bugler for his regiment. Unlike band members, who during the actual battles spent most of their time carrying out medical duties, buglers and drummer boys were right in the middle of the fighting, providing a communications network in the field decades before wireless communication was invented. They were essential for effective maneuvership in battle—a dangerous role that formed a vital component of military strategy.

Such were the duties of a military bandsman in the Civil War—music-making similar to that created in peacetime, but performed under the most extreme and often harrowing of circumstances, with actual battlefield experience thrown in for good measure. If Lavallée thought joining up would be a lark, he was eventually disabused of that notion, as were so many other Civil War recruits.

Calixa Lavallée's war was very real.

...

It started out relatively peacefully. Although Lavallée talked very little about his experiences in the war in later years, we can travel right beside him in the Union army thanks to an extraordinary memoir written by Corporal George H. Allen of Company B of the Fourth Rhode Island Volunteers, Lavallée's regiment. In *Forty-Six Months with the Fourth Rhode Island Volunteers, in the War of 1861–1865: Comprising a History of Its Marches, Battles, and Camp Life*, Allen documents his war service from its beginnings in October 1861 to its end in April 1865, and through his diary we can follow him and Calixa Lavallée in quite astounding detail.

Allen enlisted in the Fourth Rhode Island at almost exactly the same time as Lavallée, in early September of 1861, and together they headed to Camp Greene, that temporary camp where thousands of recruits were assembled just outside of Warwick, the result of an enormous recruiting drive that had swept Rhode Island in the fall of that year. This would be Calixa Lavallée's first taste of army life. It was deceptively serene. The camp was a scene of tremendous excitement as more soldiers arrived every day; they were a focus of attention not just for the other soldiers but also for the local populace, who trooped out daily to see the boys in their sharp, new blue uniforms.

Life in Camp Greene was undoubtedly enlivened by the band of the Fourth Rhode Island, as the group entertained the troops and most likely the many visitors as well. The camp was the first time many of the recruits had ever been away from home. For the farm boys among them, who had probably never seen more than two or three hundred people assembled together before, the shock of seeing a regiment of one thousand, a division of nine thousand, an army of fifty thousand, all assembled in one place and at one time, must have been overwhelming.

The "vacation" at Camp Greene ended after a couple of weeks, and Lavallée and the Fourth Rhode Island were sent by boat and train to Washington, D.C., along with all the other Rhode Island volunteers. They were to be part of the immense and famed

Army of the Potomac, the chief fighting force for the Federal side, which comprised soldiers from throughout the North, from Massachusetts and New York and Pennsylvania and Rhode Island and Ohio and Connecticut—hundreds of companies, regiments, and divisions, close to 150,000 troops altogether. All assembled to fight the Confederacy, to preserve the Union, to save for the future the democratic unity of the Republic.

Lavallée had been in Washington before, as part of Duprez's troupe, but for most of the Rhode Island recruits, this was their first view of their country's capital. The train taking them from Baltimore went interminably slowly until "cries of 'Washington!' 'Washington!' resounded through the cars," as Allen records, "and all eyes were peering forward to get the first glimpse of our nation's capital." But what Allen and his comrades saw was not what they expected:

> We were soon greeted with the first view of the huge, half-finished dome of the Capitol building, looming high in the air not far away, and began to get our traps together, ready to disembark. . . .
>
> Being the capital of our great and glorious country, we had expected to see marble palaces, splendid gardens, and parks adorned with statuary and fountains. . . . Fancy our surprise at seeing so few large buildings, no parks or fountains, . . . [but] plenty of low, flat, or shed-roofed houses . . . plenty of filthy mud and pond holes, with plenty of ducks, geese, hogs, and dirty juveniles wallowing therein.

Camp life for the Fourth Rhode Island Regiment in Washington was far different than it had been in Rhode Island. Their new camp—Camp Mud, they called it—was cold and damp, and the odd monotony of wartime became a reality for Lavallée and his comrades. In the first month of the regiment's stay in Washington, as they awaited their next assignment, they marched to and fro, met new regiments, went to the White House to be inspected by President Lincoln, were reviewed by the commander of the Army of the Potomac—Major General George McClellan, or "Little Mac"—and were officially mustered into the Federal army on October 30, 1861, approximately six weeks after Lavallée had signed up for duty in Providence. If Lavallée had expected great glory and excitement as a soldier and a bandsman, he would have been sadly deflated upon his arrival in Washington. Boredom, maybe even regret, was more likely the order of the day.

Lavallée and Allen had to wait two more long months before active duty beckoned. The Fourth Rhode Island remained in camp in Washington and the surrounding area until January of 1862. Finally came the long-anticipated order to move out. The Fourth Rhode Island were to head for the North Carolina coast as part of a campaign led by Ambrose Burnside, the Rhode Island general who was later to become so famous among Civil War commanders. Because so many of the great battles of the Civil War were encounters on land—Gettysburg, Shiloh, Bull Run, among many others—we forget how important naval operations were to the war, especially at the beginning of the conflict. Maintaining a naval blockade of Southern ports was key to the overall Federal strategy: it cut the South's trade links to Europe and restricted imports to its communities. Capturing forts that overlooked Southern harbours was essential to maintaining the blockade. President Lincoln had been persuaded by George McClellan that attacking those forts from the sea as well as by land would be a successful strategy. So General Burnside had been chosen to lead a force of twelve thousand Union troops on a naval expedition to close down the Confederate ports on the North Carolina coast. Lavallée's Fourth Rhode Island was among the regiments chosen for the expedition.

Their transport was an amazing affair. Forty-six different vessels—a motley array of steamers, paddle ships, whatever could be pressed into service—were assembled just to carry the soldiers for the expedition, with several other vessels added for ammunition, supplies, and the horses that pulled the wagons and cannon of the army. A fleet of twenty gunboats also joined the campaign.

On January 9, the expedition was ready to depart, and Lavallée and his comrades' long wartime preamble was finally at an end. There was great excitement among the troops, who were anxious to escape their camp-life solitude and servitude. "At 10 o'clock," George Allen recounts, "at the report of the gun, [we] weighed anchor, and we broke out into cheers and shouts, while our musicians of the band blowed to the extent of their lungs, and our steamer proudly swept on down the bay with all colors flying." The sight of the departing fleet, he writes, "filled our young hearts with enthusiasm."

The cheers of the Fourth Rhode Island were short-lived, however, as within two days, violent storms off the North Carolina coast mercilessly battered the enormous fleet. Several of its supply ships were destroyed, including the *Pocahontas*, which had been carrying stores, supplies, and over one hundred of the Fourth Rhode Island's horses. Only nineteen survived. After this calamitous beginning and several succeeding storms, Burnside's enormous army stayed on board its many ships for a full month to recover, awaiting orders to start the campaign. Finally they came and "immediately this great mass of vessels that had lain so quietly for the past month, became a scene of activity and animation, as the crew of each vessel heaved at the windlass or brought their anchor home on the run. The graceful moving of the various vessels to their place in the line of advance, the music of the bands enlivening and cheering our hearts . . . at once inspired us with feelings of patriotic fervor, and all we desired was a chance to strike a blow in behalf of our country's flag."

So noted George Allen.

The fleet's objective was the capture of the fortifications on Roanoke Island, at the north end of Pamlico Sound. After two days and nights moored in the sound, the day of conflict arrived and the fleet made its way towards its fortress destination. As the boats moved up the sound, the guns of the Confederate artillery, positioned both on shore and on ships in the water, showered their deadly shells on the gunboats leading the Federal troops. George Allen was on one of those gunboats, facing combat for the first time in his military career. "It [was] glorious," he later wrote.

While Allen attacked the enemy from the water as part of the gunboat fleet, Lavallée and the rest of the Fourth Rhode Island marched towards Fort Defiance on land. Burnside's forces eventually scored a victory at Roanoke Island, as they would do again a month later at New Bern, and a month after that near Morehead City, forcing the capitulation of Fort Macon on the North Carolina coast. At the end of the battle, Joe Greene and Calixa Lavallée led the Fourth Rhode Island band triumphantly into the captured fort, with Federal forces following behind. It must have been a memorable occasion.

The Fourth Rhode Island had joined the war. Lavallée and his comrades had finally seen action and had spent a victorious, and not that costly, three months facing a real enemy. The campaign had been a success, and the regiment spent a comfortable eight weeks in Beaufort, North Carolina, keeping the peace and continuing their training. They took part in Fourth of July celebrations in that town, where, Allen notes, "the band [closed] the exercises of the day by turning out in antique costume, and marching through the town, playing all sorts of—anything but music—to the great amusement of soldiers and citizens, and the uproarious delight of the colored population." Lavallée for a moment might have thought he was back on the minstrel stage.

However, things were about to change for the Fourth Rhode Island. Although Burnside's expedition had been a success and had won him a promotion to major general, things were not going as well up north. On July 3, in Beaufort, a rumour spread among the Union troops that Richmond had been taken by the Federal army, a major victory. People took to the streets in jubilant celebration. Only the next day was it revealed that, far from taking Richmond, McClellan's forces had suffered a striking defeat there and were heading back to Washington to lick their wounds and regroup. Things had gone especially badly when a new general had taken over the Confederate command in the middle of the campaign— one Robert E. Lee. To bolster the faltering Union forces as they made their ignominious way back to Washington, Burnside and seven thousand of his troops were hastily ordered back north. The Fourth Rhode Island were among them. They left North Carolina just two days after those Fourth of July celebrations.

What Lavallée and his regiment couldn't have known that July day was that they were inexorably headed towards one of the most decisive encounters in the entire war, a single day's battle that would engulf them and literally change the history of the United States. It wouldn't come for a few months, but they were months of great anxiety for the North as Robert E. Lee began his aggressive command of the Confederate army, setting the stage for his dramatic assault on the Union—an audacious attack on Union soil, a pre-emptive bid to end the war once and for all in one great encounter.

It would all come down to a single day's horror, on a swath of peaceful, rolling Maryland countryside wedged between the Potomac River and a tiny, meandering creek—the Antietam.

...

It is remarkable enough that Calixa Lavallée, the author of Canada's national anthem, fought in the U.S. Civil War at all. For him to have been present at the Battle of Antietam is doubly so—it was as if he had fought at Trafalgar, or Waterloo. The Battle of Antietam is one of the most significant events in the history of North America. It was the battle that gave rise to the Emancipation Proclamation, making it perhaps the turning point in the entire Civil War. Many historians feel Antietam, not Gettysburg, was the battle that eventually ensured Union success.

But for Calixa Lavallée and the tens of thousands of other men who were thrown into the Battle of Antietam, it had another meaning entirely—as a charnel house of unimaginable proportions. This bucolic rolling countryside, an area just four miles long and a mile and a half wide, was the scene of the single blood- iest day in American military history. For just about twelve hours on Tuesday, September 17, 1862, approximately ninety thousand men—along with their cannon, muskets, and horses and caissons, surrounded by rampaging and terrified livestock maddened by the noise—faced off and set about trying to destroy each other as efficiently and thoroughly as they knew how.

And they were brutally successful. Twenty-three thousand men were either killed, wounded, or missing when the darkness of night forced the Battle of Antietam to an exhausted end. That's the equivalent of over thirty casualties a minute—one every two seconds—for twelve consecutive hours. Eight thousand men were either wounded or killed just in the battle's first few hours, in Miller's Cornfield. That's more than the number of casualties American troops suffered on all of D-Day. By noon, another 5,500 men had fallen a few hundred yards south at Hog Trough Road, a depression worn in the earth by years of taking animals to market (and known since Antietam as Bloody Lane). Later in the day, there was more heavy fighting further south, near Rohrbach Bridge over Antietam Creek, now known as Burnside's Bridge after the Union general who stormed it time and again with disastrous consequences.

By most accounts, Calixa Lavallée was one of the twenty-three thousand wounded at Antietam. He implied so himself, and many other writers have made the same claim, although his war records make no mention of this fact. How serious the wound, no one knows, but he did spend several weeks convalescing in southern Maryland following the battle. He was nineteen—a child, really, caught up in one of the bloodiest military days in history.

Lavallée and the rest of the Union army found themselves at Antietam because Robert E. Lee was a born gambler, and an audacious, daring, almost irresponsible general. After his victory defending Richmond against George McClellan's superior forces, Lee had decided to do the totally unexpected—attack the North on Northern soil. For some, then and now, this was the height of foolhardiness. Attacking an army that outnumbered you almost two-to-one on its home turf seemed a sure recipe for destruction.

But there was much method in Lee's madness. He knew that the Northern advantage in manpower and supplies meant that the longer the war continued, the more likely it was that the South would lose. The North would simply wear it down. So, gambling on an early knockout blow—a decisive, unexpected Southern victory on Northern soil—actually made sense. Lee also knew that Abraham Lincoln led a far less unified country than many supposed. A lot of Northerners simply wanted the war to end and to make peace with the Confederacy. A big Southern victory would embolden those Northerners. And finally, Great Britain, always happy to see the United States falter, was just about ready to announce its support for the Confederate side in late 1862, which would have enormous international consequences. A great Confederate victory in Maryland might make it happen.

And so, in the first week of September, without waiting for Jefferson Davis's permission, Lee marched his Army of Northern Virginia across the Potomac, invading Maryland, hoping to entice the North into a response. As anticipated, he got it. George McClellan had been assembling an enormous army in Washington, expecting to have to defend the capital, but now he moved it out across Maryland to counter Lee's maneuvers. Calixa Lavallée was part of this immense, sixty-thousand-strong force, with his Rhode Island regiment having been recalled from South Carolina specifically for an occasion just like this one.

Lee, on the offensive, had the early advantage in what became known as the Maryland Campaign. But, incredibly, two Union soldiers taking a break in their march towards Lee's army found a copy of the order that Lee had sent to his generals outlining his entire campaign strategy. At first, McClellan thought the order, which the soldiers had found in a field, wrapped around two cigars, was a forgery—it was too outlandish that his opponent's strategy should be revealed to him so easily—but he eventually took it for the true document it was. All of a sudden, Lee was in trouble; McClellan knew exactly where he was headed. The Union army turned towards South Mountain in Maryland in pursuit. Lee fell back and considered abandoning the campaign altogether, heading back home to avoid a complete disaster. But he liked the layout of the terrain just west of Antietam Creek; its rolling hills and forests seemed perfect for the construction of tough-to-penetrate defensive positions. He stopped there, set up his artillery, positioned his forces, and waited. It was September 16, 1862.

Late that night, in the rain, Calixa Lavallée arrived at Antietam. He and his regiment were positioned just on the other side of Antietam Creek, at the far southern end of the battlefield. Confederate forces were so close at hand that Lavallée and his comrades had to set up camp in the dark. Any light would have immediately drawn enemy fire. No band concerts or diversions this evening. Instead, an anxious, wet, rainy night.

Lavallée and his regiment camped beside a little bridge that spanned the Antietam, just one hundred and twenty-five feet across and twelve feet wide. The idea was for Burnside's forces to cross the bridge at first light and attack the Confederate army from the south while other Union forces were joining the battle from the north, crushing Lee in the middle. Calixa Lavallée was ready to be among the nine thousand men who would cross that tiny bridge under heavy Confederate sniper fire and bombardment. He may well not have survived—thousands were killed or wounded trying to cross that span during several attempts over a three-hour period.

But Lavallée was spared that crossing. Early in the morning, Burnside sent the Fourth Rhode Island on a mission to outflank the Confederate snipers guarding the bridge by fording the creek a mile downstream and sneaking up behind them. The maneuver was supposed to take an hour but ended up taking six. (The maps they had been provided were wildly inaccurate.) Six hours of trying to make their way through dense underbrush, lugging artillery behind them, fending off the occasional sniper fire and artillery blast. Finally, at about four in the afternoon, Lavallée and his comrades, having made their way across the creek, appeared just to the west of Burnside's Bridge, ready to join the battle.

And join the battle they did. While Lavallée was fording the Antietam, Burnside had finally gotten the rest of his forces across, and the final phase of the battle was about to begin. By this point in the day, tens of thousands of men had already been killed or wounded on the Antietam field, but the battle still hung in the balance. The Fourth Rhode Island started advancing towards the town of Sharpsburg, where Lee had set up his headquarters, and were making great gains. It looked as though Antietam was going to be, finally, a Union victory. But at the very last moment, in a scene right out of Hollywood, a new supply of Confederate troops, who had marched all day to get to Antietam when it was clear they would be needed, streamed onto the battlefield exactly where Lavallée and the Fourth Rhode Island were fighting their way to Sharpsburg. Had the Confederate troops arrived a half hour later or half a mile distant, they would have had no effect whatsoever. As it was, they caused chaos for Calixa Lavallée and his comrades. Fighting fresh and superior forces, the Fourth Rhode Island eventually had to retreat after a vicious battle in what is now referred to as the "forty-acre cornfield." The regiment lost fifteen men in that brief, intense battle (by way of comparison, they only lost twelve other men during the entire rest of the war).

And in that cornfield, Calixa Lavallée himself was wounded. The nature of his injury is not entirely certain, although many sources from his later life say it was his leg. Leg wounds were common during the Civil War because exploding shells would cause rock fragments to act like shrapnel. Whatever the nature of the injury, it was serious enough to necessitate a convalescence of several weeks. And it ended his wartime career. A year in the army, spent under the most harrowing of circumstances, reaching its climax on the fields of Antietam, was over. Although Lavallée spoke little of his wartime experiences in later life, they scarred him as they scarred everyone involved in that conflict. The man who would write the national anthem for his country saw at first hand the agonies of another country facing the trauma of its possible dissolution. It was a haunting vision of disunity he would never forget.

FOUR

EXACTLY TWO DAYS AFTER Calixa Lavallée was mustered out of the Union army following his post-Antietam convalescence, he presented himself at Charles Duprez's doorstep once again, ready to resume his duties with Duprez and Green's New Orleans Burlesque and Metropolitan Opera Troupe and Brass Band. He clearly had arranged to rejoin Duprez while he was still recovering with his army comrades near Sharpsburg. He travelled to Providence to put on the burnt-cork makeup, get back into the band, and be a minstrel once again.

It was the fall of 1862; he was nineteen. The war had been a year-long episode in his life, but he was ready to resume the life he had led before he enlisted. The restricted and provincial narrowness of Montreal—or, worse, Saint-Hyacinthe, were not for him. Lavallée still wanted to play music, and his immediate opportunities in America seemed more real than the distant opportunities—if there were any at all—in Quebec. For three years now, he had been living and travelling and fighting in America—it had become, perhaps, a sort of home for him. So, for another year, he continued his peripatetic American life, not to return to Montreal until December of 1863, four years after he had first left at sixteen.

Had he returned home in 1862, he might have been surprised, even shocked, at the impact the War of Secession was having on his native country. We Canadians don't think the Civil War had much to do with us. It is something that happened in another country—something important, but not part of our history. But without the Civil War, Confederation might never have happened. Almost certainly, it wouldn't have happened when it did—the talks to bring it about would not have begun in Charlottetown in 1864, while the war was still raging. And the Civil War had a profound impact on the way we chose to structure our Constitution.

But if the Civil War was having an effect on Canada, equally significant, and surprising, was the fact that Canada was having an effect on the Civil War—we were far from mere observers of the conflict. And it wasn't just because an astounding number of Canadians, as we've noted, enlisted as combatants. From the citation of the Quebec Act in the Declaration of Independence as one of the "Intolerable Acts" that led the Americans to seek their own country, to the War of 1812, to the Fenian raids of the 1860s and 1870s, Canada has always had a role to play in the story of the American republic. The Civil War was no different.

Canada played three major roles in the hostilities. In the first place, we were from the beginning a potential zone of armed conflict in the war, a constantly looming second front that neither we nor the United States government could ever quite ignore. We were threatened more than once with possible invasion during the war, and we feared that prospect even more once the conflict was over and a standing Union army of six hundred thousand men had nowhere to go but north. In the closing months of 1861, during the "Trent Affair," war between Britain and the United States seemed so imminent that ten thousand British troops were hastily dispatched to Halifax.

Secondly, we hosted a rogue's gallery of Southern sympathizers and Confederate spies throughout the war—Montreal and Toronto in particular became hotbeds of subversion and espionage—that did real damage to Northern interests. We were a constant thorn in the Union's side. Further, as a British colony, we were part of an international diplomatic web of influence and intrigue that figured quite prominently in the strategic military decisions made by both North and South. Foreign influence in the war was far more significant than most Americans realize.

And finally, we were part of the Civil War here in Canada if for no other reason than that John Wilkes Booth, Lincoln's assassin, was in Montreal months before the assassination, may have planned the deed with associates in Canada, had money withdrawn from a Montreal bank in his pocket when he fired his pistol in Ford's Theatre, and was almost assuredly heading for Montreal when he was cornered and killed in a New York State barn.

Canada thus had a deeper—and more complex—relationship with the Civil War than one might think. We now proudly assume that right-thinking Canada was firmly on the side of the slave-liberating North during the war, and opposed to slavery's defenders in the South. The reality was much more complex. There was a surprisingly deep level of support for the South in this country, especially in the early days of the conflict, especially among the country's elites.

It seems shocking now. When the first victory of the Confederate army, at Bull Run, was announced in the Canadian legislature in 1861, spontaneous cheers of joy broke out on the floor of the House. It took the Speaker several minutes to reassert control. Of the one hundred and seventeen newspapers in Canada at the beginning of the war, only thirty-three supported the Union. Eighty-four were pro-Confederacy—over 70 per cent.

Part of Canada's affection for the South was simply a reaction against a too-powerful North, and a too-powerful United States in general. It was part of a deep-seated sentiment in British North America that held that anything that weakened the United States strengthened Canada. And also removed a clear and present danger: the threat of an invasion of Canada by United States forces, especially if they were newly triumphant over a rebellious South. We forget how real that possibility seemed in the 1860s and 1870s. Lincoln's secretary of state, William Seward, was an especially strong and vocal proponent of manifest destiny, the notion that the United States was fated to occupy the entire North American continent, and President Lincoln could never quite get around to censuring Seward in a timely fashion. The fear of such expansionism powerfully played into the creation of Confederation in 1864 and 1865.

But there was more than simply a reaction to a powerful North at the heart of Canadian support for the Confederacy. In some ways, British North America was mimicking the attitudes of Great Britain itself in the early days of the conflict, with its skepticism of the North and its clear preference for the cotton-producing South, which supported the enormous British textile industry. Britain toyed with supporting the South for a long time, and the Southern strategy in the war, right up until Antietam, was to convince Great Britain (and France as well) to enter the war on the Confederate side. The Confederacy had a very receptive audience to this notion in Westminster and Paris.

Canadian attitudes towards the Civil War had a deeper source as well. Certainly in Quebec, especially among Church officials and provincial politicians, there was great sympathy for the South and its cause. The Church in particular consistently sided with the Southern plantation owners. It wasn't that the Church was pro-slavery (although slavery existed throughout the eighteenth century in both Upper and Lower Canada), but rather that French Canadians, or at least their leaders, saw themselves reflected in the tribulations of the Southern rebels of the Confederacy. Here was a group of people with a traditional way of life and a traditional economy completely different from that of the Protestant, industrial North, asserting their independence with pride and force of arms—American separatists, in a sense. How could Quebecers not see a version of themselves in this context? They were, in effect, a northern mirror image of the beleaguered South, the two societies both forced against their will to give up their hallowed and deeply felt way of life in the name of modern values they did not share. It is no surprise, really, that many official institutions in Canada were very much on the side of the South when the war began, especially in Canada East.

What is equally noteworthy is that most ordinary Canadians felt exactly the opposite of their so-called opinion leaders. Of the fifty thousand British North Americans who enlisted in the Civil War, the vast majority joined the Union side, by a margin of ten to one. And public opinion in Canada was heavily in favour of the North. The institution of slavery, so loathed by the general populace, provided a compelling and ultimately overwhelming stimulus for Canadians to oppose the Confederacy. Canada had always been a part of the racial conflict in the United States because of its terminus position on the Underground Railroad. Canada was "the other side of Jordan"—freedom—for so many black Americans. So there was a significant section of the Canadian population that was powerfully abolitionist. Despite their dalliance with rebel independence to serve whatever political and religious self-interests they might have had, Canadian opinion leaders never managed to convince the average citizen to follow them. And the same split between the government and the public existed in Great Britain. There stands in Manchester to this day a statue of Abraham Lincoln, built to commemorate a letter that the people of the city, despite hurting desperately because of the lack of Southern cotton, nonetheless sent to the president supporting his anti-slavery cause in the war. Lincoln's reply, remarking on the Mancunians' moral courage, is one of the most famous documents of the war.

If Canada was acutely ambivalent on the edge of the conflict in the United States, with the sympathies of its citizens falling one way and the attitude of its government another, its geography implicated it in the conflict more thoroughly than anything else. In a geographical sense, it was a boon to the South. Montreal and Toronto were the Casablancas of the Civil War, close to the action but uninvolved in the actual conflict. If you were a Southern agent, what better place than British North America to spy on the North? Within a hundred miles of the enemy, but protected from prosecution by Canada's official neutrality. But the South did more than just keep tabs on Northern fortunes through its friends in Toronto and Montreal. Agents of Jefferson Davis were constantly hatching and launching incursions into Union territory from north of the border—some successful, most not, but all a constant annoyance and worry for the Union government. The fact that the Confederacy had many supporters in British North America didn't hurt these efforts, either. Cassius Lee, Robert E. Lee's cousin, lived out the entire war in Hamilton, Ontario. Jefferson Davis himself came to live in Montreal for a few years as a form of exile after the war. And there were many other Southerners who spent considerable time in Canada during the war. Perhaps meeting with Southern agents was the purpose of John Wilkes Booth's visit to

Montreal six months before the assassination of President Lincoln. We shall never know. But that both Toronto and Montreal were rallying points for Confederate espionage and sabotage is beyond question. Far from the battlefield, the country that Lavallée had left behind was exerting an influence on the war, as real as the saxhorn he had been playing in the Union army for almost exactly twelve months.

. . .

The world of minstrelsy that Calixa Lavallée returned to in the fall of 1862 was a different place than it had been a year earlier. Perhaps he had expected it to be unchanged by the war, but that was not to be. During the year Lavallée had been in the army, Charles Duprez had avoided the United States entirely, instead spending six months in British North America, in Newfoundland and the maritime provinces. Not surprising, given that minstrelsy was based on a rough amalgam of radical politics and racist tropes, too sensitive by far to be let loose in a nation convulsed by the early days of the war. But when it became clear that the war was not ending quickly, Duprez realized he couldn't stay in exile forever and decided to go back on the road for the 1862–63 season. Perhaps his receipts in Canada had been too meagre. Perhaps he felt that he could maneuver his way through the sensitivities of the conflict with more assurance in 1863 than he could have when the war began. For whatever reason, Duprez made his decision, and when Lavallée rejoined the troupe in October of 1862, it was with the assumption that the group would resume the kind of schedule and itinerary it had followed before the war.

It wasn't easy. Just getting around the country was difficult for a large group of performers and stagehands, with troop movements clogging roads and hotel rooms hard to come by. But more significantly, the social and political climate in which the minstrel show had operated with such surefootedness in the past was now turbulent and unpredictable. Minstrel troupes now needed to think, for the first time in their history, about presenting different shows for Northern and Southern audiences. Inevitably, the political content of the minstrel show, so important in the pre-war years, began to recede in significance during the conflict itself, of necessity, causing considerable changes in the internal lineup of the shows. All of a sudden, instead of his comedians and satirists commanding top billing, Duprez now felt he could draw the crowds with "Signor Monteverde, the Great Spanish India Rubber Man" as his headliner. He had also increased the role of music in the show now that Lavallée was back with the troupe, and the latter was constantly writing new arrangements and compositions for the show. With all these adjustments, Duprez was ready to hit the road again with renewed success, war or no war.

The New Orleans Minstrels stayed mainly in the Northeast in the fall of 1862 before heading down to New Orleans in December for an extended stay as they had done in the past. But New Orleans was now a forlorn Southern metropolis. About ten months earlier, the city had been occupied by Northern forces, and the occupation had often been brutal. A Federal blockade of ports in the South was also eating away at the once-boisterous Southern economy, and New Orleans was feeling the pinch. Business began strongly for the show in early December, but it eventually started to weaken so much that Duprez and Green were forced to temporarily team up with another minstrel company. The star performers of that company, which was managed by William Ellinger, were two dwarves, Commodore Foote and Colonel Small. The combined troupe stayed in New Orleans for a month or so, until January 24. It was a marriage of convenience that eventually would have significant implications for Lavallée and his career.

Duprez may have thought he had solved the questions of social content in his show, but for the first time in his career, Duprez ran into political controversy while in the South, amid charges that his troupe was sympathetic to the Union and the North. It was true to an extent. While in the North, still the show's most important audience, Duprez had responded to public taste by providing many war-related songs and sentimental battle scenes, all attuned to the sensibilities of the North. "The Dying Young Hero"—the hero in question being Northern—was one of their biggest new numbers. Not unsurprisingly, the war broke apart the subtle, complex mechanisms that had made minstrel shows such a powerful mode of social cohesion in the United States in the pre-war years. Minstrelsy forever lost its ability to meld together disparate political views and would never again occupy that subversive, bawdy, shady corner in American political and emotional life. After the war, it became more mainstream, more family-oriented, less political, more conservative. The war broke minstrelsy's subversive heart.

And so it was that, on his way back north, Duprez did not wend his way through several southern states as he had done for the fifteen previous years. With the war raging all around them, he, Lavallée and the troupe headed directly back to Newark from New Orleans, and travelled west instead. In the spring of 1863, they went to Chicago for the first time, as well as to Madison, Dubuque, Indianapolis, Cleveland, Rochester, and Buffalo. The show also toured extensively in Canada again, this time in what is now southern Ontario and Quebec: Toronto, Wentworth County, Hamilton, London, Ottawa, Quebec City, and ten full days in Montreal.

Lavallée hadn't been home for almost four years when Duprez's troupe set up residency in Montreal. It must have been with the keenest of conflicted emotions that he returned to his native province—not as a famous classical performer, as he might have once imagined, but as a gyrating American blackface minstrel. His family were still living in Saint-Hyacinthe. Did he tell them he was in Montreal? Did his fans and patrons who had known him as an up-and-coming serious musician know he was performing with the Great Spanish India Rubber Man and Commodore Foote? We know that minstrelsy was immensely popular in Canada—witness the ten-day run in Montreal—so one assumes that Lavallée's Canadian visits were well received. Yet it's not hard to imagine that his minstrel years were a source of deep and abiding pain to Lavallée, especially when, a few years later, he was finally able to rebrand himself as a serious musician.

Even with his disastrous New Orleans run, his twisted travelling schedule, and the trials and tribulations of running a minstrel company in watime, Charles Duprez must have felt a certain satisfaction as he "rusticated" as usual, in Providence in the summer of 1863, and prepared for the fall season. But he was going to have to do so without Calixa Lavallée. Lavallée had left Duprez's band and taken a job with William Ellinger, the impresario with whom Duprez had formed a short-term partnership the previous winter in New Orleans. It was the first time in his minstrel career that Lavallée had ever worked for anyone other than Charles Duprez. But as musical director for Ellinger and Newcomb's Great Moral Exhibition, Lavallée had opportunities more exciting than his former duties as bandleader, composer, and arranger for Duprez. The Great Moral Exhibition was still a minstrel show, a variety extravaganza now featuring three diminutive performers instead of just two, but its attraction for Lavallée may well have been that one of its regular features was the presentation of a parlour opera that Lavallée would get to arrange and conduct, without the need of blackface. Ellinger was also planning a trip to Europe with his outfit. Both of these were presumably enticing draws for the young musician.

Although Lavallée stayed with Ellinger and Newcomb for just a few months in the fall of 1863, his desire to work with them seems to reveal a central and defining conflict in his life. Lavallée was obviously a highly skilled popular musician—dozens of reviews and informal comments attest to his prowess as a performer, arranger, and composer. As well, he was more than able to hold his own personally in the tough, hurly-burly, Wild West world of the blackface minstrel show—the most competitive popular entertainment of the mid-nineteenth century. But something else burned inside him: the desire to be a serious, classical musician, with something important and profound to impart to his society. This contradiction surfaced time and again in Lavallée's life, tossing him back and forth between his two worlds without either claiming him. The fall of 1863 was the first of these psychological and professional upheavals when Lavallee put aside the minstrel life and began again a serious music career.

For Lavallée, pursuing a career in classical music always meant returning to Quebec, and so back he went to Montreal in December of 1863. He had not felt the need to return home after his war service ended and he had instead happily rejoined his minstrel colleagues on the road. Now, just a year later, and mere weeks before his twenty-first birthday, something had changed. Maybe the ten days that he had spent in Montreal with Duprez's troupe in the spring had whetted his appetite for his native country, but for whatever reason, in the midst of what seemed to be a highly successful run with Ellinger's Great Moral Exhibition,

Calixa Lavallée suddenly gave up the minstrel life he had lived for three years and returned home. Since he had left, he had seen and experienced a great deal more than most twenty-one-year-olds of his time, or of any time.

Le Canadien errant was returning. But not, as it turned out, for long.

FIVE

THE MONTREAL TO WHICH Calixa Lavallée returned in December of 1863 was substantially different from the city he had left in 1859. At over one hundred thousand inhabitants, Montreal was by far the largest urban centre in British North America, and the ninth-largest city anywhere on the continent. Just under half of its citizens were French; just under a quarter were English. Musical life in the city was progresssing quickly with its increasing population—there were regular concerts, a few well-known players, a just-developing audience for serious music, and an equally nascent music-education establishment.

But Canada as a whole was still very much a backward colonial outpost in the mid-nineteenth century, despite the fact that Confederation was not far off. Both Upper and Lower Canada, now Canada West and Canada East, were still close to their rugged pioneer pasts. Art, music, literature, and theatre were cultural sophistications that sat uneasily in societies just a generation or two separated from their log cabins and seigneurial farmhouses. And in Quebec, the heavy hand of the Roman Catholic Church, a devotional fog blanketing the intellectual life of the entire province, also weighed profoundly on artists and their potential audiences.

The Church was suspicious of music, of theatre, of entertainment in general—of anything that might distract parishioners from their complete, godly immersion in the faith. It was not the most inspiring atmosphere for an artistic mind and soul like Lavallée's, especially a soul now hardened by three years on the road in a top-flight minstrel show and a year under fire in a Civil War regimental band. It is no surprise that the Montreal of 1864 and the ambition and talents of a twenty-one-year-old Calixa Lavallée did not immediately and completely mesh.

Lavallée rejoined his family at the beginning of 1864—it was the first time he had lived with them in almost a decade. Papa Augustin had moved his organ and instrument repair business from Saint-Hyacinthe to Montreal and was beginning to specialize in the construction of violins. He eventually would become the most famous violin maker in Quebec; his shop was a meeting place for musicians in the city for decades. Lavallée set himself up as a music teacher upon arriving in Montreal, and also started giving concerts in the city. A number of new performing spaces had opened up since his departure in 1859, and there seemed to be an increasing array of musical possibilities for this returning prodigy.

Lavallée resumed his Canadian musical career with a flourish, presenting four different concerts in January 1864 alone. Although he sometimes appeared with cornet and violin, he increasingly featured the piano as his main instrument. He wrote many of the compositions he performed, a testament to the remarkable amount of composing and arranging he had done on the minstrel circuit. His *galop de concert* "War Fever," written for Duprez, was a special favourite. But Lavallée's musical life in Quebec was radically different from the performing career he had just left. In Montreal, he abandoned his life as a popular musician and concentrated almost exclusively on classical music. This change of direction would prove temporary, however, and he soon returned to his old life. However, his ability to remain true to his two wildly different musical personas would eventually buckle and weaken, until he finally gave up the minstrel life altogether, ten years later. Although he never spoke on the issue, the split must have caused him great inner distress. Here is a performer and composer with a serious musician's heart and soul, from the backwoods of Canada in the mid-nineteenth century, forced by circumstance and economics to seek his fortune in the dark but exciting underworld of popular music. He is successful but unsatisfied in this life, which he finally, after great struggle, abandons. It is a tale that has been retold in North America many times during the past century or so, but Lavallée represents one of its earliest manifestations. He is the ultimate artist born ahead of his time.

Still, his return to Quebec allowed Lavallée to finally exercise the talents and musical tastes he had had to suppress during his minstrel and war years. And he took full advantage of his opportunities. For Montreal's Saint-Jean-Baptiste Day concert in June of 1864, a major musical event, Lavallée was everywhere. He conducted the band in the overture to Verdi's *La traviata*; accompanied a tenor singing a cavatina from Bellini's *Norma*; played the "Grande marche triomphale" from *Aida* on the piano; led the band again in his own composition, "Les quadrilles canadiens"; and finished by playing excerpts from Gounod's *Faust* on the piano. Not a bad evening's work—and evidence of what a remarkable force this talented young Québécois musician represented in the middle of the 1800s. Indeed, it's hard to imagine any other Canadian musician within a century—French or English—who could have pulled off what Lavallée accomplished in 1864 with such versatility and skill.

Lavallée continued his musical activities throughout 1864. He performed regularly, mostly for charitable purposes, though occasionally for cash. He began to do music reviews for *L'union nationale*, a radical Montreal newspaper, and continued to teach during the fall of 1864 and the spring and summer of 1865. Most importantly, he formed a couple of very strong personal and musical friendships during the two youthful years he was in Montreal— one with the orchestra leader, pianist, and journalist Charles-Gustave Smith, the other with the violinist Frantz Jehin-Prume. With both of them, Lavallée would have long and fruitful associations. Jehin-Prume was a young, talented musician just like Lavallée, and the two struck up an immediate friendship. The violinist was originally from Belgium and had only arrived in Montreal in the summer of 1865, but in the short time he and Lavallée spent together (they would reunite several years later), they were a force to be reckoned with. Jehin-Prume was as accomplished a violinist as Lavallée was a pianist, and the two together made music of a superior quality. Jehin-Prume's gorgeous tone and impassioned playing were matched by Lavallée's virtuosity and sweep at the keyboard. Montreal had certainly not heard music-making of this quality before, and never from musicians based in the city itself. It was a novelty that Montreal wasn't prepared for, however, and the audiences for the two musicians' joint concerts were disappointingly small. Like so many other provincial centres, Montreal was still a young and innocent musical community when Jehin-Prume and Lavallée swooped down upon it in the 1860s, a town still overly impressed by second-rate travelling ensembles strictly because they were from somewhere else. Lavallée noted the phenomenon in one of his newspaper columns. "Poor Montreal," he wrote in one review for *L'union nationale*, "when will you stop being overwhelmed by such itinerant opera troupes? Are you so poor in artists that you must receive with open arms the mediocrities other countries send you?" This was a theme he would return to several times in years to come.

For all of his activity in 1864 and 1865, Lavallée began to tire of life in Montreal and to despair at the thought of staying in Canada. Some of that frustration was musical, but just as importantly, he seems to have been profoundly alienated by political developments in Canada during these two years. Of all the transformations that Lavallée was going through back in Montreal, it is perhaps his political consolidation that was most significant.

Calixa Lavallée was a musician, not a politician, but he took a substantial interest in the political affairs of his society. He was, after all, to write its national song. And at the end of 1864 and the beginning of 1865, Quebec was embroiled in perhaps the most significant debate in its history—the controversy surrounding the Confederation of the British North American colonies to create a new country, the Dominion of Canada. Although we normally associate Confederation with the passage of the British North America Act of 1867, the key discussions in Canada about this new political configuration actually took place in the preceding years. Lavallée was in Quebec for the entire process; he saw it all at first hand.

Today, we assume Confederation was accepted with equanimity and excitement, but the truth is that in Quebec, the debate around the proposal was heated and extremely divisive. Only 55 per cent of French Canadian Members of Parliament voted for Confederation in the Canadian legislature, likely reflecting the views of the French population as a whole. Confederation divided the province almost equally. It was the first Quebec referendum.

The idea of a union of the British North American colonies had been in the political air for about a quarter century or more by the mid-1860s, both as an expression of natural geographical unity and as a bulwark against the threat of incursion by the United States. That threat had been ramped up significantly by 1864, as the Civil War was coming to an end and a Union victory was all but assured. But beyond the fear of actual invasion, it was clear to leading Canadian politicians of the time, especially John A. Macdonald, that a newly unified United States would necessitate a similarly unified northern political organization to stave off the increasing political, economic, and cultural power of the Republic. The Dominion of Canada (originally to be called the Kingdom of Canada) was at one and the same time a political and military necessity, the creation of a new nationality, and a bet on the future, an unknown adventure in the history of North America.

But for many francophones in the province of Quebec, the cost of that new nationality seemed to be the annihilation of their own culture, history, and being. It was to be a form of radical cultural erasure, creation of a frankly and baldly English nation that would stretch from sea to sea. Confederation meant that they—along with their past glories, present reality, and future prospects—were to be sacrificed in the name of the Dominion. An English Dominion. They felt it was too high a price to pay. Calixa Lavallée agreed with them.

And, as we shall see, it was precisely to celebrate that imperilled culture and to protect Quebec from future political despoliation that "O Canada" was to be written fifteen years later. In many ways, the seeds of that anthem—that passionate French Canadian hymn to the glories of the past and the future of la patrie—were planted in Lavallée's heart in the mid-1860s, in Montreal, during the Confederation debates.

The notion that French Canadians viewed Confederation as complete cultural annihilation may seem extreme to twenty-first-century Canadians. But Lavallée and Quebecers of his generation had some very real evidence on which to base their existential fears. And they came from an unlikely source, at least to the minds of English Canadians: the pen of John George Lambton, 1st Earl of Durham, the author of the famous 1839 Durham Report.

English Canadian historians give Lord Durham a remarkably wide berth concerning the frankly racist statements about French Canadians in his report because he is, for them, the father of responsible government, that form of uniquely Canadian governance that still forms the basis of our democratic and parliamentary traditions. Responsible government allowed a dependent colony to start its advance to a modern state, and Durham's understanding of this need for representative democracy, quite radical and far-seeing for its day, has blinded many to the other, more questionable aspects of his report.

But not in Quebec. To this day, Durham remains one of the most hated figures in the history of the province. For French Canadians of Lavallée's generation, he represented everything they most feared about English colonial domination, with his outspoken call for French national destruction, and his enthusiasm for, and insistence on, a completely homogeneous, English, sea-to-sea dominion on the northern half of the continent. French Canadians had been holding their breath, fearing a figure like Lord Durham from the moment of their conquest by the British in 1760. For eighty years, they had been spared such a spectre; finally, they were not.

John George Lambton was sent to Canada in 1838 to help the British government respond to the Rebellions of the year before in both Upper and Lower Canada. As we noted earlier, although the 1837 uprising in Upper Canada was a generally tame affair (Durham spent almost no time in that province during his travels), the battles in Lower Canada and their aftermath were significant. Three hundred and fifty people, from both sides, were killed during the Lower Canada Rebellions, which ultimately spread over two years. Figuring out what caused them, and how to prevent similar crises in the future, was a major priority for the British government.

Durham expected to find a typical nineteenth-century political conflict when he got to Canada: a conservative, anti-democratic governing elite, looking backwards and defending outmoded privilege, confronting a popular, democratically elected assembly, progressive and forward-looking, embracing the future. And in Upper Canada, that's more or less exactly what he discovered.

But in Lower Canada, Lord Durham was surprised. The traditional opposition of conservatism and progressivism was mysteriously reversed. In Lower Canada it was the oligarchs, the commercial class, the so-called Château Clique, who were the progressive forces trying to push the colony into the future. And it was the democratic popular assembly which was the conservative party, stubbornly and blindly resisting change. Something didn't make sense; something more fundamental in the politics of Lower Canada was at play. Durham dispensed with conventional wisdom and discovered, or so he thought, what we would now call a clash of civilizations—two deeply divided groups in the province, each coalescing around ethnicity, with fundamentally and irreconcilably different value systems.

"I expected to find a contest between a government and a people," Durham famously reported. "I found two nations warring in the bosom of a single state: I found a struggle, not of principles, but of races; and I perceived that it would be idle to attempt any amelioration of laws or institutions, until we could first succeed in terminating the deadly animosity that now separates the inhabitants of Lower Canada into hostile divisions of French and English."

French Canadians, he observed, led by their Church, stressed continuity and conservatism in their lifestyles and political choices.

They were agricultural, rural, rooted in their historical relationship with the land. The English commercial class, on the other hand, was bustling and progressive, and eager to exploit the land and its resources for new profit and gain.

Two nations warring in the bosom of a single state. Perhaps the most famous single line in Canadian history. Everyone knows it. But few in English Canada are familiar with Durham's proposed solution to the "deadly animosity" he found in Lower Canada.

It was to simply and completely eliminate French culture in Lower Canada, to destroy it once and for all. The inhabitants of Lower Canada, he said, "resemble rather the French of the provinces under the *ancien* regime" with their "backwards laws and civilization." He concluded that "there can hardly be conceived a nationality more destitute of all that can invigorate and elevate a people, than that which is exhibited by the descendants of the French in Lower Canada. . . . They are a people of no history, and no literature." Harsh words, routinely quoted in French Canada today. And more than likely engraved on the minds of Calixa Lavallée's generation. Durham continued:

> I entertain no doubts as to the national character which must be given to Lower Canada; it must be that of the British Empire; that of the majority of the population of British America; that of the great race which must, in the lapse of no long period of time, be predominant over the whole North American Continent. . . . It must henceforth be the first and steady purpose of the British Government to establish an English population, with English laws and language, in this Province, and to trust its government to none but a decidedly English Legislature.

In other words, a nonviolent ethnic cleansing; a program for the elimination of a language, a culture, and a community. An "extinction of a nationality," as he called it. For the generation that included Calixa Lavallée, who was born just after the report was written, Lord Durham's words provided a constant reminder of the potential threat to their culture and language, a permanent source of mistrust and hostility towards the increasing English majority of the country. Lavallée's entire political outlook, and that of his generation, was forged upon the smithy of Lord Durham's cultural annihilationism. Lord Durham made Calixa Lavallée, and others like him, a Quebec patriot.

Of course, Lord Durham's chilling and patronizing words had the exact opposite effect to the one he intended. Rather than speeding along its dissolution, Durham accelerated the development of a French Canadian culture that had lain somewhat unexpressed before his report. In the 1840s, it sprang to fulsome life, specifically to prove him wrong. The first history of French Canada, a three-volume affair, was written in 1845 by François-Xavier Garneau as a direct response to the claims of cultural nullity that Lord Durham had made in his historical overview of French Canada. French Canada did not just roll over and play dead. Faced with potential annihilation, it responded with stubborn resistance, determination, pride.

Durham's scheme for eliminating French culture was a political one. He recommended creating a single, united province of Canada out of the old Upper Canada and Lower Canada, to be divided into two sections, Canada West and Canada East. The point of the unification was to allow the English populations of both sections—an enormous majority in Canada West, and a sizeable minority in Canada East—to form a permanent alliance in the united province. Against that alliance, French Canada would be overwhelmed, constantly outvoted by the English majority. The French language, French law, French custom, and the protection of the Catholic religion could thus progressively be eliminated. And with no provincial governments included in the new scheme, there could be no recourse for French-speaking Canadians looking for an alternate power base for protection. It was cultural dismemberment by "democracy."

Durham's recommendation was acted on by the British government—the 1841 Act of Union put precisely that scheme in place. For twenty-six years, before Confederation replaced it, that was the strange interregnum in Canadian politics that no one today really understands: of Canada West and Canada East, of no provincial governments, of a moveable capital—a regime primarily intended to destroy French Canada.

And although Confederation was to replace the United Province of Canada with a different governing structure, Calixa Lavallée and his compatriots were equally suspicious of the new plan—their patriotism had been put on alert by Lord Durham and the Act of Union, and it wasn't going to be easily mollified. To them, Confederation was just a more sophisticated version of Durham's scheme, with the same ultimate goal. Yes, Quebec recovered its autonomy and became a province again under the proposed plan, and yes, the provinces were to be given some specific powers. But it was clear to the opponents of Confederation that these powers were mere window dressing. Based on speeches they heard and read by people like John A. Macdonald (always delivered in Ontario, never in Quebec), it was clear that the entire point of Confederation was to create a strong, powerful central government that would be the real force in the new Dominion. The provinces were afterthoughts. And that central government was going to be completely and utterly English in its orientation, heart, mind, and soul. "A British subject I was born, and a British subject I shall die," Macdonald was eventually to say. And people like Calixa Lavallée took him at his word. Confederation, they believed, was designed to create a British Dominion in the northern half of the continent, and the puny powers that Quebec would have were not intended to deny that British character one whit. It was Lord Durham redux. Its intent was the same—to corral, if not destroy, French culture in Canada. It must be stopped if Quebec was to have a vital, continuing future.

So a very dedicated and powerful set of opponents emerged in Quebec against the Confederation proposals—men like a young Wilfrid Laurier; Gustave Smith, one of Lavallée's closest musical associates; and especially Médéric Lanctôt, a fiery young journalist who in 1864 left the newspaper he had founded, *La presse*, to create a brand-new one, *L'union nationale*, totally devoted to opposing Confederation. Although Lavallée never spoke publicly on the issue, he was a friend and colleague of all of the most prominent Confederation opponents. He advertised his piano teaching services in *L'union nationale* and eventually ended up writing music reviews for them. He clearly was on their side.

However, the opponents of Confederation were never quite able to bring their fellow citizens around to their point of view. The conservative proponents of Confederation constantly reminded Quebecers of the new powers the province would receive under the proposed plan, to prove that Quebec would gain, not lose, autonomy in the new federation (even though these new powers were repeatedly dismissed as irrelevant in speeches John A. Macdonald gave outside of Quebec). It was a difficult argument to counter. And when the Church came down heavily on the pro-Confederation side, the game was basically up. In March 1865, the legislature of the United Province of Canada voted overwhelmingly in favour of

Confederation, 91–33. Among its French Canadian members, the vote was much closer, 27–22. But in both linguistic groups, a majority approved the new scheme.

Although Confederation would not be made official until July 1, 1867, its opponents wasted no time in registering their disgust with the new proposal; they left Quebec soon after the March 1865 vote was taken. Calixa Lavallée was one of them. Frantz Jehin-Prume returned to New York, where he had previously lived, in November. Gustave Smith took up a post in New Orleans. Louis-Honoré Fréchette, Quebec's leading poet and a bitter foe of Confederation, left for Chicago. Médéric Lanctôt managed to hang on until 1868 before he, too, departed. Even Wilfrid Laurier, the anti-Confederationist who eventually became prime minister of the country, went into a form of exile, leaving Montreal for Victoriaville for several years.

Lavallée himself only stayed in Quebec until the fall of 1865, six months after the Confederation vote. The lure of the road, and of the minstrel life, claimed him again. It's not clear that his decision was entirely political; had he been doing better as a teacher and performer, making more money and establishing himself more thoroughly in the province, the Confederation vote alone would probably not have triggered his decision to leave. But that he was an opponent of Confederation, seeing it as a threat to his nationality and a scheme to restrict the French fact in Canada, was never in question.

Thus, we must confront the very specific Canadian irony that the author of our national anthem was steadfastly opposed to the creation of the country that took his composition as its symbolic song. The new nation neither fired Lavallée's imagination nor won his political allegiance. Outside of two visits he made to Ottawa, totalling maybe five days together, Lavallée never set foot in the rest of the country post-Confederation. He spent more time in Canada West in blackface as a touring minstrel than he ever did in Ontario as a legitimate musician. Lavallée was interested in the cultural life and history and future of Quebec, of French Canada. That was his "home and native land." Confederation made the future of that land much more difficult to determine.

And artistically, Lavallée was simply ahead of his time. What he wanted to do as a performer, composer, and conductor in the new Quebec ran far ahead of the opportunities which the culture of a very rudimentary, albeit growing, province offered him. His bursting talent just didn't fit the restrictive opportunities that the Quebec of the 1860s placed at his disposal. His departure had always been a possibility. As early as January of 1865, articles had appeared in the Montreal press exhorting people to support Lavallée to keep him in Montreal.

They were to no avail. Lavallée, still young and restless, felt that the ties binding him to his homeland had grown weaker than ever. The lure of the road—of money, fame, excitement, and musical challenges—beckoned. Once again, he heard the siren call of Charles Duprez and the world of minstrelsy. Once again, he left Canada to tour and travel through the United States as leader of a minstrel band.

This time, however, it wouldn't be for a season or two but for a substantial period in his life—a kind of exile. Lavallée left Montreal towards the end of 1865, when he was twenty-two. With one exception, he would not return until he was almost thirty.

SIX

CHARLES DUPREZ MUST HAVE been overjoyed to have Calixa Lavallée back in his band. Although he was initially rehired as a simple musician, it only took Lavallée a few weeks to return to his familiar position as musical director of the troupe. He hit the road in January of 1866. There had been a change in the organization of the New Orleans Minstrels while Lavallée had been in Montreal. Lew Benedict, the show's tenor, had bought out John Green, so Duprez and Green had become Duprez and Benedict, eventually one of the most famous minstrel troupes in America, performing well into the 1880s.

With the political controversies of his home province behind him (Confederation wouldn't actually come into effect for a year and a half), Lavallée returned to the mid-1800s equivalent of a rock star's life for the next couple of years, travelling from big city to small town, prancing and gyrating in blackface every night, playing the violin, piano, and trumpet. Offstage, he was just as busy, arranging music for the increasing number of opera parodies that Duprez and Benedict included as part of their standard show. Minstrelsy lost a great deal of its pre-war edge in the late 1860s, instead starting its long march towards respectability, which would eventually result in the more family-oriented vaudeville show of the 1890s. That change was needed to reflect the realities of the Civil War and the post-war world. The South, devastated by the conflict, was no longer a site of imagined idyllic pleasure for audiences up North, and black Americans, now freed, no longer so easily served as potential objects of ridicule, humour, and mockery. The very foundations of minstrelsy had been ravaged by the war and its aftermath. But Lavallée soldiered on, and he was extremely successful in the minstrel business. More and more of his compositions were published and featured on the minstrel-show bill, as fewer of the troubles and frustrations of his home country clouded his view.

Duprez and Benedict, with Lavallée leading the band, followed the troupe's usual performing itinerary for the rest of the 1866–67 and 1867–68 seasons, with tours that took them throughout the northeastern and western United States and into Canada as well, but not in the South. Duprez had stopped touring there several years earlier. Lavallée was actually in Canada just a few weeks after Confederation was proclaimed in July of 1867, but the country likely would not have recognized him behind his blackface as he journeyed through Hamilton, Kitchener, Ottawa, Montreal, and Quebec City. (Lavallée was never mentioned by name in advertisements for Duprez's troupe in Quebec.) He was enjoying the lifestyle of the travelling entertainer, it seemed, and was content with his busy and exciting life.

But just a year later, in the summer of 1868, as Duprez and Benedict ended their run for the season, Lavallée up and quit the company and headed back to Montreal.

There were probably several motivations for Lavallée's decision, not the least of which was his long-standing desire to immerse himself in serious music. But perhaps more significant was the fact that, in December of 1867, a week before his twenty-fifth birthday, Calixa Lavallée had gotten married. The bride was Josephine Gentilly, a young French–Canadian woman from Lawrence, Massachusetts. Her family was part of the enormous French Canadian diaspora in the northern United States; both her brother and her father had been killed in the Civil War. Calixa and Josephine probably met in early 1866, almost two years before their marriage, when Duprez and Benedict were performing in neighbouring Lowell. The troupe didn't return to Lowell again until October of 1867, and whether Josephine and Calixa met somewhere else during that time is unknown. Either way, at this point, things heated up between them, and Charles Duprez seemed to help play matchmaker for his talented bandleader. After his October visit, Duprez didn't wait two years to return to Lowell, as he had the last time the troupe had performed there. The group showed up again just six weeks later, in mid-December, and then just a week after that, on December 21— specifically, it seems, so Josephine and Calixa could get married.

Which they did, that afternoon. Lavallée was back on stage that evening.

Josephine joined Duprez's travelling entourage with her newly minted husband starting in January of 1868, but we're not sure exactly how long she stayed. She seems to have gotten pregnant almost immediately after their marriage, and was expecting when Lavallée quit Duprez's troupe and headed back to Montreal. It's certainly possible that it was her pregnancy and the prospect of a family that convinced Lavallée that life on the road was no longer for him, although Josephine did not accompany him to Montreal when he returned there in the summer. She went back to Lawrence, where Calixa Jr. was born in October. Calixa Sr. was hundreds of miles away at the time.

Josephine and Calixa's life together is one of the most obscure and confounding parts of his biography. Although they remained married until his death in 1891, they were separated for long stretches of time during the marriage. Josephine occasionally accompanied Lavallée on the road, but most of the time she was left behind. Lavallée spent two years in Paris without her; he moved to Quebec City for over a year and a half in the 1870s and left her in Montreal; and routinely we hear of her in Lawrence or Lowell during his many years on the road. When he eventually moved to Boston, she stayed behind in Quebec for many years. They actually spent more of their married life apart than together. Still, they managed to have four children, only two of whom survived beyond infancy. Perhaps Lavallée's economic circumstances prevented the family from living together more frequently; perhaps there were other factors. (Of Lavallée's sex life we know nothing, although it's hard to imagine he remained celibate travelling with a minstrel troupe through post–Civil War America, where prostitutes routinely plied their trade in the second balcony during the shows.) One way or another, in Lavallée's biography, Josephine passes as a shadow, a hint of a presence lurking behind the main activity of his life.

Such was the case when Lavallée returned to Montreal in the late summer of 1868, with his pregnant wife about to give birth back in Massachusetts. It seems to have been a joyous homecoming. Lavallée was greeted with immense enthusiasm by the musical public, as the returning prodigal son. Two major concerts featuring him as pianist, conductor, and composer were immediately arranged. The first, held in September, was the inaugural event of the newly opened St. Patrick's Hall, testifying to the importance the Montreal musical community bestowed on the young musician. Lavallée was to give another at St. Patrick's later in the month. The two concerts were universally expected to be the first of many in the city. In fact, they turned out to be his last in Montreal for almost five years. His "triumphant return" to the bustling Quebec metropolis lasted all of two months.

That's because the siren song of Charles Duprez, the road, and minstrel life was never far from Lavallée's conflicted heart. He had abruptly quit Duprez's show in July; Duprez had advertised for his replacement in August. But by September, Duprez had ensnared Lavallée once again. The wily minstrel leader had even decided to open his season that year in Montreal, bringing his entire troupe up north to ensure that his wayward bandleader wouldn't stray again.

Lavallée's past and future collided in Montreal that September. Two notices, placed one above the other in Montreal's *Le pays* newspaper that month, tell the story all by themselves. Both advertised musical events, to be held on two successive nights, a Wednesday and a Thursday. Lavallée was involved in both.

The Wednesday event was Lavallée's second concert at St. Patrick's Hall, a massive affair he had organized himself that featured him conducting an orchestra, leading soloists, and playing the piano. The Montreal papers were full of news of the event. "Everyone is talking about the grand concert to be given by our Canadian artist, Mr. C. Lavallée," reported *La minerve*. It was a major musical event in post-Confederation Montreal. And a major artistic success.

But the next night, at Mechanics' Hall, for quite a different audience, Lavallée was leading another orchestra. The audience would have had to look carefully to recognize "our Canadian artist" behind the blackface and the hijinks and the vulgarity of the "degenerate" New Orleans Minstrels. The middle-class and polite audience of Wednesday had given way to a raucous and working-class crowd. And, one assumes, the *La minerve* critic who had rhapsodized about Lavallée's playing on Wednesday would have been scandalized to find Lavallée leading performers in blackface singing fake plantation songs on Thursday.

In that collision of Lavallée's past and future, just as he approached his twenty-sixth birthday, his past won out. Lavallée gave his well-received major personal recital on the Wednesday and on Thursday was back with Duprez. By Sunday, he had left Montreal behind and was back on the road. In Lawrence, Josephine gave birth to their first child, Calixa Jr., on that very same day. Lavallée was in Ontario. He remained far from Quebec, both spiritually and physically, until the beginning of 1873. When he finally arrived back home those five years later, it would be with the intention of burying his minstrel past as thoroughly and completely as possible. For now, however, the lodestone of Montreal and its community was not strong enough for him to cling to.

Lavallée was again successful as a minstrel. His unique gifts as performer, conductor, arranger, and composer made him a highly sought-after figure on the circuit. With Duprez's new postwar touring schedule, the New Orleans Minstrels spent more of their time in the Northeast and the Midwest than in the South. But what might have been an exhilarating schedule of touring for Lavallée when he was seventeen and eighteen now started to become wearing as he entered his late twenties. Travel was not easy, requiring a combination of steamship, train, and wagon. Like all touring troupes, Duprez and Benedict's company had to carry their sets, costumes, props, and instruments with them. They would set up in a new town, perform one or two nights, then be off again. And Duprez had scheduled a punishing itinerary for the 1868–69 season. Over the course of the next twelve months, the troupe, starting in Montreal, headed to Ontario, Michigan, upstate New York, Connecticut, Rhode Island, Massachusetts, New Jersey, New York again, Maryland, Pennsylvania,

Ohio, Indiana, Kentucky, and Tennessee, then back through Indiana and on to Illinois, Minnesota, and another tour of the Midwest before alighting, finally, in Philadelphia in August of 1869. A full, uninterrupted year's worth of travel for a not-so-young Lavallée, with a wife and child far from him, must have been exhausting.

And it wasn't just the travelling and performing that would have occupied Lavallée's attention. With minstrelsy's attempts to become more family-friendly, more appealing to women, less raunchy, and more smoothed-out, the role of music in the show increased exponentially. In addition to performing in and leading the band, Lavallée was writing sentimental songs to serve as the foundation of this new version of the minstrel show, as well as arranging and rehearsing the elaborate opera burlesques that formed the glittering finales of each night's performance. One of these in particular achieved considerable success. It was a parody, in blackface, of Patrick Gilmore's National Peace Jubilee, a major concert of brass bands that took place in Boston in the summer of 1869. Gilmore was the most famous bandleader in the United States in the generation before John Philip Sousa—his band had been one of the most prominent during the Civil War—and the Peace Jubilee was advertised all over the country. Lavallée's parody, which featured a takeoff of Verdi's "Anvil Chorus" from *Il trovatore*, was so popular that Duprez kept it in his repertoire for two years.

But despite the successes coming his way, Lavallée clearly needed a more permanent lifestyle. He found what he was looking for—or so he thought—at the beginning of 1870, when he again jumped ship, leaving Duprez and joining the San Francisco Minstrels, one of the most famous troupes in the history of minstrelsy. Despite their name, the San Francisco Minstrels were permanently based in New York, with a dedicated theatre for their performances. The North and New York in particular had always been the home of minstrelsy, and in 1870, a New York–based troupe like the San Francisco Minstrels would have been a nation-wide leader. Lavallée's accession to music director was a major event in the business.

Again, following his now well-rehearsed pattern, Lavallée was quite successful in his new post, especially in the composition of the opera parodies that had increasingly become the focus of the postwar "modern" minstrel show. And again, one in particular created quite a stir, this time a parody of a real New York character: James "Jubilee Jim" Fisk, a three-hundred-pound, larger-than-life, Donald Trump–like figure who had once cornered the market on gold, and who ran a successful railway (however unscrupulously) and operated two major theatres in New York. Fisk drifted in and out of scandal, both commercial and sexual, throughout his career, and in 1872 he was murdered by a jealous husband in his railroad offices, above one of his theatres.

Fisk had produced an enormous spectacle for one of his theatres just before his death called *The Twelve Temptations*, full of lavish sets and scantily clad actresses and with a cast of hundreds—a forerunner to the Busby Berkeley and Cecil B. DeMille film extravaganzas of the decades to come. It was a major success. Eager to capitalize on such a controversial spectacle, Lavallée wrote a parody of the show, featuring a figure based on Fisk himself, called *The Thirteen Temptations, or Fisk Raised One*. It was a hit for the San Francisco Minstrels for several seasons.

Despite Lavallée's success in New York, he took up an offer to move to Boston to join the Morris Brothers Minstrels in the summer of 1871. By this time, he had also composed an operetta, called *Peacocks in Difficulties* (or *Lou-Lou* in French). Although it was never produced and is now said to be lost, it did get positive reviews from people who had seen the score and libretto. It may have been the basis for Lavallée's first produced operetta, *The Widow / La veuve*, written ten years later.

Moving from a nationally famous minstrel troupe to a less well-known regional outfit was uncharacteristic for Lavallée, as was his move away from New York, minstrelsy's unofficial capital. It seems to speak to Lavallée's fatigue and weariness with the minstrel life. He was now six months shy of his thirtieth birthday; he had spent the better part of his life on the road, since age sixteen. It's also possible Lavallée wanted to be closer to his wife and child, assuming they were still living in Massachusetts. As well, he may well have wanted to re-immerse himself in more serious music—a need that constantly tugged at him, demanding to be recognized— and Boston was far and away the most important city in the United States for classical music.

Lavallée quit the Morris Brothers show after just one season (that made three companies for him in just two years), but after he left the troupe, he stayed in Boston to try to start a career as a serious pianist. He performed Mendelssohn's G minor Piano Concerto with Hall's Band, one of Boston's leading ensembles, in December of 1872, along with a Chopin mazurka and several of his own compositions. It's fascinating and a little tragic to think of Lavallée, on tour with Duprez, or in New York with the San Francisco Minstrels, stealing a moment here and there—maybe before he "blacked up" for the evening performance, maybe on an off day, or a touring day—hauling out his scores of Mendelssohn and Chopin, sampling their sophisticated artistic beauties, and reflecting on the distance between them and the sounds he was making every night in his raucous, populist shows. How sick was he of the smell of burnt cork as he rubbed it on his hands and face every night? How tired was he of the life of a common minstrel entertainer? Lavallée never once spoke of these experiences, so we can only speculate. But, judging by the evidence of the rest of his life, he clearly realized that it was time to remake himself, time to become who he wanted and needed to be. Time to come home.

So, in January of 1873, Lavallée returned to Montreal. His minstrel life was finally a thing of the past, and he was determined to lay it to rest once and for all.

Lavallée started this quest to remake himself in two quite different ways. First, he arranged for a gala concert for himself in March of 1873. It was the talk of musical circles in the city for weeks. Montreal never forgot Lavallée, for all his travels and absences. And in preparation for that concert, he gave an interview to an old friend from the pre-Confederation days, Laurent-Olivier David, who was now working for the weekly newspaper *L'opinion publique*.

The article David wrote was the first comprehensive look at Lavallée's career that had ever been published in Canada. It contains many biographical details about Lavallée's life, presumably supplied by the musician himself, that have lain at the heart of most Lavallée biographies ever since. You can find them still in the *Dictionary of Canadian Biography*, the *Encyclopedia of Music in Canada*, his Wikipedia entry, and in several other publications. Some of these details were routinely cited in the House of Commons debates on establishing "O Canada" as our official national anthem. They constitute the official Lavallée biography. And, with a few exceptions, they're all lies.

Lies that David made up for his readers, or, more likely, lies that Lavallée made up for David—lies, exaggerations, obfuscations, and half-truths that he found necessary to tell to create the story of his life that he desperately wanted to present to the Canadian public.

Lavallée told David that he had been made an officer in the U.S. Civil War. Not true. He told him that he had been accompanying the violinist Jacques Oliveira (spelled Olivera in the article, a misspelling which endures to this day) in South America and the West Indies after he first left Montreal in 1859. Not true. He implied that he had been travelling and performing alone throughout the United States for years. Not true. He told David he had been commissioned to write an operetta for Jubilee Jim Fisk, which was cancelled, abruptly, on Fisk's murder. A good story. But untrue. He said Fisk had hired him to be the "superintendent" of his Grand Opera House. None of it true.

In almost every case, Lavallée's lies were told to hide a truth he clearly did not want the Quebec public to know—that he had spent the better part of ten years in blackface. Lavallée felt he had to hide his participation in a "low" entertainment business that he knew his middle-class audience would find degenerate and immoral, especially the elders of the Church. He believed his past must never be allowed to conflict with his desire to recreate himself as a serious musician. Surely there were many Montrealers who knew of his minstrel career, but he nonetheless persisted in protecting his secret, never once speaking of that part of his life— and, with willing accomplices, he managed to erase that chapter completely.

Still, there seems to have been a residue of personal pain for Lavallée attached to that riotous and vulgar musical endeavour in which he had spent a decade of his life. Perhaps it pained him because he had excelled at it. However, the desire to become a classical musician, one who could elevate and inspire his audiences and his fellow citizens, was an intensely powerful need within him. He had to fight to achieve it. And to Lavallée's great credit, he made that transformation, through long years and steady, determined effort. The years between 1865, when Lavallée first left Montreal to rejoin Duprez's minstrel band, and 1875, when he returned home from a time of study in Paris, finally a serious classical musician, were the years when this great change took place.

Lavallée's transformation was helped along by the good offices and pocketbook of none other than Léon Derome, the Montrealer who had first discovered Lavallée as a kid of twelve and brought him to Montreal to study in 1855. Now, in 1873, Derome wanted to ensure that the talented and experienced Lavallée would take the next step in his professional development. And that meant studying in the centre of classical music in the Western world—Paris. For the better part of 1873, Derome and those whom he could convince of Lavallée's talent collected the funds that would allow the pianist and composer the chance to study in an uninterrupted manner for a couple of years. Lavallée supplemented these funds with revenue from some of his concerts. In the summer, he worked in Massachusetts on the Fall River steamship line, playing for customers out on a summer evening excursion. Finally, in September, he was in the French capital, where he would spend the next two years. Josephine and Calixa Jr. stayed back in Montreal.

The march that took Lavallée out of the tumultuous world of the minstrel show and swept him towards the composition of the national anthem of his country had begun in earnest.

SEVEN

Paris was just recovering from one of the darkest periods in its history when Lavallée landed there in the fall of 1873. The Siege of Paris had ended the Franco-Prussian War in early 1871, with the French capital starved into submission by the victorious Prussian forces. During the siege, French citizens were forced to cut down the trees on the Champs-Élysées for fuel. They ate the animals in the Paris zoo. France had suffered one of the most ignominious defeats in its history. The Second Empire had come apart. Chaos ruled the streets. The suppression of the Paris Commune uprising in 1871, in the wake of the siege, had cost anywhere from twenty thousand to one hundred thousand lives.

Still, Lavallée wrote that he had expected to find Paris in ruins when he arrived, but he didn't. Instead he found a city working its way out of the destruction and devastation, both physical and moral, of the previous three years.

Although we have no diaries or records of Lavallée's time in Paris, other than a few newspaper columns he wrote for a newspaper back home, there is no doubt that the two years he spent in the French capital were among the most significant of his life. He came to Paris a provincial, musically untutored, with a chequered professional past, more experienced in the world of entertainment than in that of classical music. He left Paris a serious, national musician, trained by the finest teachers in the world, confident and sure in his musical trajectory. For the next sixteen years of his life, until his death in 1891, his path was clear. Despite the many obstacles he was to face, he never again swerved from his calling as a classical artist.

Lavallée studied both piano and composition in Paris, and his teachers were among the most celebrated in France. His primary reason for travelling to France had been to study piano with Antoine-François Marmontel, the leading piano pedagogue in the country. Paris had been the epicentre of the piano for decades—it was the home base of Chopin, Liszt, Thalberg, and virtually every other major virtuoso of the nineteenth century. And Marmontel was the go-to guy for serious students of the instrument. He had taught Georges Bizet, the composer of *Carmen*, in the 1850s. While Lavallée was studying with him, Marmontel was also teaching such soon-to-be-famous musicians as Vincent d'Indy; Isaac Albéniz, aged fifteen; and a twelve-year-old Claude Debussy.

Lavallée was no child when he studied with Marmontel, but a man of thirty with fifteen years of experience behind him as a professional musician. Where Marmontel was essential for Lavallée was in helping him refine his technique at the keyboard and opening his eyes and ears to a considerably wider repertoire, immersing him in the music of the more avant-garde composers of the day, such as Frédéric Chopin and Robert Schumann. Before Paris, Lavallée had chosen to perform opera transcriptions and his own compositions for his serious concerts—popular, easily accessible music that would please the relatively unsophisticated musical tastes of his Montreal audiences. But after Paris, he never played those kinds of barn-burning compositions again, instead focusing on the heart of the classical repertoire—on Beethoven, Mendelssohn,

Chopin, and Schumann. These hardly seem like radical composers today, but they were viewed very differently in the 1870s and 1880s. In fact, Lavallée received a fair amount of criticism on his return to Montreal for his insistence on including these composers in his programs. This was not music to be enjoyed frivolously, but art that demanded concentration, attention, and taste. Not everybody liked it. But it was all part of the new, dedicated seriousness that Lavallée was to apply to his art for the rest of his life.

At the keyboard itself, Marmontel seems to have encouraged Lavallée to be more expressive and lyrical in his playing, to use his technique as a means to a musical end rather than as a show in itself. Marmontel encouraged his students to spend time with singers to learn how to perform lyrically at the piano, a revolutionary practice even today. Taming the percussive nature of the piano—it's a box with hammers, after all—and making it sing more like the human voice was one of Marmontel's ideals. Lavallée seems to have taken happily to this notion, and he passed it on to his own students when he returned home.

Lavallée's composition teachers in Paris were equally famous—François Bazin and Adrien-Louis-Victor Boieldieu, both opera composers. Although less information exists about the nature of Lavallée's studies with them, it can be no coincidence that he wrote two operas of his own within the next ten years, and mounted productions of two others in his home province. Lavallée eventually became an important composer back home in North America, but he didn't write that much while he was in Paris—although one of his compositions from that period became his most famous outside of "O Canada." That was "Le papillon" (The butterfly), a wonderful piano portrait of that beautiful and elusive creature, still performed regularly around the world. Marmontel included "Le papillon" in a volume he published while Lavallée was still in Paris,

L'art classique et moderne du piano, and it's been a favourite ever since. Lavallée's other most significant composition in Paris was an overture for orchestra called "La patrie," written in 1874 but considered lost until the manuscript was rediscovered in 1990. Its first performance wasn't until 1993, 119 years after its composition.

"La patrie" (Homeland) was significant for more than its musical content. It signals perhaps the most important lesson Lavallée learned in Paris, the one idea that he carried with him for the rest of his life—the notion that music had a critical role to play in the political and emotional life of a community. Lavallée learned in Paris that music could, and must, be more than idle entertainment. It provided an opportunity for a nation to define itself and its values in an especially effective way. In this regard, there is a direct connection from "La patrie" to "O Canada." The music is not the same; however, the sentiment, the goal, the raison d'être of the two works is identical. Lavallée came to see that music could have a political and social meaning, and that using it to create civic virtue was one of its most important functions.

Lavallée learned this lesson in Paris because France was teaching itself this principle while he was there. France was digging itself out of one of its greatest-ever political and moral catastrophes in the years after the devastation of the Franco-Prussian war, the collapse of the Second Empire, and the shaky establishment of the Third Republic. It became obvious to leaders of French intellectual life that the arts must be placed in the service of rebuilding the nation's moral and spiritual fibre—and music was placed at the head of the procession. From small choral societies to full-scale operas, the making of music as a community activity, with people working together and helping one another, was seen as an analogue to rebuilding a society, and the efforts to make music a central part of France's rebuilding were extensive and impressive.

The French government led these efforts, which included accelerating the completion of the sumptuous new home for the Paris Opera (today called Palais Garnier, after its architect), subsidizing concerts and commissioning works, and providing funds for communities large and small to participate in musical activities. Concerts featuring only French composers were mounted and performed throughout the nation. France's greatest composers rushed to participate in this patriotic effort—Charles Gounod, for example, wrote the incidental music for a five-act drama based on the life of Joan of Arc, which opened to much excitement while Lavallée was in Paris. (Lavallée would later mount a production of this very opera back in Quebec.) Other composers followed suit.

The vision of music as a socially unifying and creative force, a nonviolent means to rebuild and create a nation, never left Lavallée. There is a direct line from the experiences he had in Paris to almost all of his musical activity for the rest of his life—as a performer, as a composer, but most importantly as a "national" musician. France had established a national conservatory a century earlier, during the French Revolution, as a focal point for the development of French musical technique, style, and taste. This idea of an institution that could stand at the centre of a society's musical activity fired Lavallée's imagination and, as we shall see, became one of his predominant concerns when he returned home.

But Lavallée's time in Paris was not all work. He managed to sample many of the beauties and delights of the French capital while he was there, even in its depressed state. This was Paris, after all. From his letters home and an occasional column he wrote for the French-language newspaper in Fall River, Massachusetts, we know that Lavallée participated eagerly in the musical life of Paris, perhaps the most musically active city in the world at the time. He attended many concerts and reviewed a number of them for his column, sharpening his critical judgement and enlarging his musical tastes. He was there when the Palais Garnier opened in 1875, and may well have gone to the Opéra Comique in March of that year to see a new production by a former piano student of Marmontel's, a racy affair about a cigar-making gypsy girl who comes to a tragic end. Her name was Carmen.

Lavallée also seems to have gotten involved in the French art scene, the impressionist circle of Manet and Monet, through his association with a Spanish couple to whom he dedicated one of the pieces he wrote in France, "Souvenir de Toledo." He may also have crossed paths with Emma Albani, one of the most famous sopranos in the world at the time, when she was in Paris. Lavallée knew her as Emma Lajeunesse of Chambly, in the Richelieu Valley. Albani was the most famous Canadian musician of her generation, a favourite of Covent Garden audiences and Queen Victoria alike.

All in all, the Paris sojourn was a tremendous success for Lavallée, on both a personal and a professional level. He used his time in the French capital to sample the culture of the city, to take in its unparalleled music scene, and to keenly observe its monuments, architecture, and spirit. Professionally, in his studies with Marmontel, Bazin, and Boieldieu, he tested himself against the best in the world, and held his own. Most significantly, he let his minstrel past sink deep into the Seine—he would never dredge it up again. He had finally transformed himself into a serious artist, and he was ready to take his newfound skills and ambition back home.

In his letter bidding Lavallée adieu as he left Paris, Antoine Marmontel wrote, "As you return to your country, Lavallée, I bid you a cordial farewell, and wish you all the success that you merit by your constant and courageous work. I count on you to transmit to your compatriots the advice I have given to you, and which you have well appreciated. Continue to love and understand beautiful music, esteem art and artists, and prove to the envious and the detractors that you have a talent beyond all reproach."

The story of the rest of Calixa Lavallée's life is his attempt to fulfill the instructions Marmontel had provided him. He was almost thirty-two years old when he left Paris, but he had spent almost none of his professional life in his home province. Now he was ready to fulfill his destiny. What he couldn't know as he sailed back to Quebec, full of ideas and promise, was just how vicious "the envious and the detractors" were going to be. He would provide his homeland with its national song, and with many other significant accomplishments, but not without great struggle and often great disappointment.

...

Calixa Lavallée arrived back in Montreal in July of 1875 teeming with energy and determination. After his validation in Paris, the road was clear for him to become the artist he wanted to be—and might always have been. A pianist of expressive tenderness, playing the most up-to-date music; an educator hoping to build a nation's taste and expertise; a conductor of power; a musical entrepreneur creating productions of excellence; a composer of the first rank. He immediately threw himself into these tasks with his accustomed zeal, starting with his own instrument, the piano.

It was his prowess as a performer, and especially as a pianist, that had seen the most development in Paris. That aspect of his art had atrophied in his minstrel days, when he had spent more of his time as a conductor, composer, and arranger. He was anxious for his compatriots to see the new artist he had become.

Lavallée unveiled this new side of himself at a free concert he gave in September of 1875 to thank all the people who had helped support his studies in Paris. To a packed, appreciative hall, he played a chamber version of Carl Maria von Weber's *Konzertstück*, with a string quartet including his father, Augustin, accompanying him (this was the only time they ever performed together). He played next in Quebec City, followed by a rare performance in Ottawa, one of only two times Lavallée travelled in Canada outside of Quebec in his entire post-minstrel life.

And immediately it was clear to his countrymen that, during his time in Paris, Lavallée hadn't just improved as a pianist—he had completely changed his artistic direction as a performer. Lavallée's repertoire was now radically different. He was playing the pieces by Chopin, Schumann, Beethoven, Mendelssohn, and Weber that he had studied with Marmontel in Paris. Joseph Marmette, a friend and critic, wrote of one concert, "The music made me wonder if I was really in Canada. And not at a European salon. M. Lavallée played . . . in such a manner so as to prove that his talent has not been exaggerated and that he is one of our national glories." Marmette and other modern-minded music lovers may have loved Lavallée's new direction, but for the Quebec, even the North America, of their day, this was radical stuff—a type of music that didn't depend on easily remembered tunes and flashy technical displays. This was serious music, built on themes and complex harmonies and intellectual forms, and not everybody in Quebec was ready for it. And so while the critics may have appreciated it, Lavallée paid the price for this change in direction in reduced popularity and revenue. But he soldiered on unhesitatingly, convinced of the worth of what he was doing.

As 1875 came to a close, Lavallée began a busy and fruitful life of performing, conducting, and teaching, as well as directing a choir at Saint-Jacques Church. He collaborated almost exclusively with a select group of fellow performers, friends, and fellow-thinking artists—violinist Jehin-Prume, with whom he was reunited; singer

Rosita del Vecchio, Jehin-Prume's wife; and critic, conductor, and composer Guillaume Couture, who had been in Paris with Lavallée. Through a series of concerts in Montreal and Quebec City throughout 1875 and 1876, this little band of musical adventurers challenged the taste of Quebecers with their new and different repertoire, played beautifully by all accounts, and attempted to create a beachhead for sophistication and excellence in Canadian music.

Lavallée had moved back into his parents' home when he arrived back in Montreal, reuniting with Josephine and Calixa Jr., but he and his family eventually settled in their own residence. It was in the middle-class, bourgeois, English part of town, which was home to an increasing number of his pupils—evidence of his growing reputation as an educator. He seems to have been extremely busy. A photograph of Lavallée taken by the famed photographer William Notman in 1876 shows an intense, somewhat haggard Lavallée—a testament to his demanding schedule and, sadly, the stress of the premature death of his second son, Joseph, who had lived for only two months in the summer of that year.

Inspired by his experiences in France, Lavallée was determined to convince the government of Quebec to create and fund a formal national conservatory, where serious musical education could be delivered by dedicated professionals according to a comprehensive, well-planned curriculum. For him, nothing short of such an institution could ensure the proper flowering of musical art in the province. The problem was that Lavallée was yet again ahead of his time in the underdeveloped world of mid-nineteenth-century Quebec. The province was still only a few generations removed from its pioneer roots and it was simply too early, it seems, for the kind of sophisticated and cultured society Lavallée hoped to establish there. It wouldn't be until well into the twentieth century that the potential of culture as an important part of communal life would be recognized in North America—a world until then just a few steps removed from wilderness, deprivation, and the laws of nature. Simply maintaining and expanding the essentials of life were all-consuming in Lavallée's Quebec. Culture would have to wait.

But there was another factor influencing Lavallée's cultural plans for his native province, one that the rest of North America did not share: the power of the Roman Catholic Church.

The Catholic Church exerted an influence on Quebec society, from the highest levels to the lowest, that was unprecedented in North America. Catholicism was not just a religion in Quebec—it was an ideology, a political philosophy, an identity, even the essence of life itself. To be a Quebecer was to be a Catholic. The two were interchangeable.

In the years just before and after Confederation, an extremely conservative variant of Catholic thought, called ultramontanism, came to predominate in Quebec. In Europe, ultramontanism emerged after the upheavals and cultural convulsions of the French Revolution. It was fundamentally an anti-democratic and anti-secular movement, stressing the superiority of ultimate religious truth over mere man-made reality. That truth was to be found "across the mountains"—that is, in Rome and the papacy.

In Quebec, ultramontanism was used to cement the primacy of the Church in all aspects of life. By the 1870s, the Church's authority in the province was unchallengeable—and it wielded its power in the province possessively, defensively, viciously. However, with subtlety and guile, that authority could be challenged. It was not omnipotent. For an artist like Lavallée, the most significant aspect of the ultramontane ideology was its hostility to anything modern and secular—including, perhaps especially, art. To the nineteenth-century Church, the modern world was to be shunned in all its aspects. Quebec was to be a beacon among the nations as a society dedicated to simple things—to agriculture, custom, and the glory of the Christian God. Art, seen as either a frivolous entertainment or, worse, a challenge to faith as a source of truth and enlightenment, was the enemy, save for the restricted possibilities of devotional art. The Church and artistic creativity were forever at odds.

Calixa Lavallée and many other anti-clerical Quebecers held a completely different view of the nature of modern life, and of the purpose of music within it. From his time in Paris, a very secular city, Lavallée had learned to see in art rather than in religious doctrine the sinews and ligaments that bound up a nation and a people. Lavallée was certainly a nationalist, as were the Church fathers, but unlike them he believed in a modern future for his country, not slavish adherence to a restrictive past. That's why the idea of a secular, rational conservatory dedicated to the musical arts was so important to him.

It seems inevitable, then, that the values of the Church and the values of Calixa Lavallée were going to come into conflict. And they did, at the beginning of 1877.

In January of that year, the diocese of Montreal—for reasons, one assumes, of moral probity—declared an end to the use of mixed choirs in the city's Catholic churches. No longer would the sinful practice of allowing men and women to sing together in church be permitted. This edict meant that Lavallée was going to have to disband the very fine church choir he had been painstakingly building up at Saint-Jacques Church in downtown Montreal. Lavallée's hard work was about to be destroyed.

It seems it was the parish priest of Saint-Jacques, enraged by the diocesan order, who came up with the novel idea that the choir could be kept together, after a fashion, if they became the chorus in an opera—an opera that Lavallée would organize, cast, conduct, and present. The Church might object to mixed choirs, but they couldn't as easily object to an opera chorus, which was ostensibly out of its realm. Operas had been touring throughout Quebec unimpeded for years.

It's hard to imagine anything more ambitious in the Quebec of 1877 than the idea of presenting an opera made up of strictly local musicians. There were hardly any professional musicians in Quebec: Who would do the singing? Who would play in the orchestra? Who would direct the cast? Who would produce the whole thing? The notion must have seemed beyond audacious, verging on the foolhardy.

But Lavallée loved the idea, and knew exactly the piece to perform—*Jeanne d'Arc*, the five-act play with incidental music by Charles Gounod which had caused such a sensation when it had debuted during Lavallée's stay in Paris. The piece worked for Lavallée for several reasons. It was a play with music rather than an opera, so there were no solo singing parts to cast, just a chorus. That solved a big problem; the chorus was the one thing Lavallée had, thanks to the church. Further, from the play's reception in Europe, Lavallée knew it could be a success. And perhaps most importantly, the Catholic Church could hardly object to an enterprise based on the legend of the heroic and devout Joan of Arc. Who would dare say no to a five-act portrayal of the life and martyrdom of France's greatest religious heroine? *Jeanne d'Arc* it would be.

With only a few months in which to mount the piece, Lavallée threw himself into the frantic preparations. He held intensive rehearsals to teach Gounod's heavenly music to his choir-turned-chorus. Then, with money from benefit concerts, and perhaps additional funding from Léon Derome, Lavallée prepared an orchestra, hired a stage director, oversaw the construction of sets, and attended to all the details of a major operatic production. He found his Joan in Rosita del Vecchio, the one highly accomplished singer in the province, here making her acting debut. The amount of work and effort he lavished on this production was monumental, and surprising to many. But he had an ulterior motive. If *Jeanne* was a success, it could prove to the skeptics that Quebec had a well of musical talent that would benefit from more professional training, and Lavallée's conservatory project might come one step closer to reality.

Jeanne d'Arc was indeed a great success when it finally opened in May of 1877, running for six performances in the spring and another dozen in the fall. *La minerve* called the production "a dazzling success." The *Canadian Illustrated News* noted that "the representation was equal to that of many theatrical companies which we have had here, and superior to several others." It was a personal triumph for Lavallée, with his skills as a conductor, coach, chorus leader, entrepreneur, and impresario all prominently on display. But more importantly for him, it was also a truly historic moment: Quebec's first homegrown opera production. As Lavallée never failed to mention, all the musicians in the production were Quebec natives, even if most were amateurs. No longer, Lavallée felt, did Quebecers need to import their musical talent from afar. As well as presenting a serious work of art to the public, *Jeanne d'Arc* was intended to prove to a recalcitrant government and Church that a national musical conservatory in Quebec would have many potential students and prove its worth several times over. Just ten years after Confederation, Lavallée thought he could see the future clearly for musical taste and instruction in the province.

But *Jeanne d'Arc* did not immediately rouse the conservative forces in government to action. Nor would any reasonable person have expected it to. However Lavallée had a vision, and he was never one to give up easily. So, for both artistic and political reasons, he and his colleagues decided that *Jeanne* should be followed by another Quebec-produced operatic extravaganza, with the same long-term goal in mind.

This time, Lavallée chose a complete opera rather than a play with music, and an especially popular one: *La dame blanche* (The white lady), an adaptation of two stories by Sir Walter Scott written by French composer François-Adrien Boieldieu (Lavallée had studied composition in Paris with his son). *La dame blanche* was the most successful opera in French history at the time, with more than a thousand performances to its name in France alone. (*Carmen* would eventually dethrone it as the most popular French opera ever.) And with its Anglo-Saxon origin in the work of Scott, Lavallée felt that *La dame blanche* had the capacity to interest both the French- and English-speaking communities of Montreal. Once again, Lavallée trained his chorus, assembled an orchestra—this time also coaching his soloists—oversaw the construction of sets, assembled and organized and inspired the whole enterprise. He contracted Marietta Hassani, a veteran of European opera houses, to sing the main female role, since Rosita del Vecchio, his first choice, was by then pursuing a career in Europe. The production opened on April 22, 1878.

It was another roaring success. Reviews were positive, with many critics expressing astonishment at the quality of playing in Lavallée's pickup orchestra, given that the players were all amateurs. Unlike *Jeanne d'Arc*, *La dame blanche* was also presented in Quebec City (where one critic noted that it was "a chaste and delicate entertainment," unlike the province's "still-popular minstrel shows") before Lavallée brought the production back to Montreal for a second run, making for an extraordinarily large number of performances—sixteen in all—for the relatively tiny province. Both *Jeanne d'Arc* in 1877 and *La dame blanche* in 1878 buttressed Lavallée's belief that there was exceptional talent in Quebec, and an audience for first-rate musical fare.

Of course, the Quebec City performances of *La dame blanche* were part of the plan that Lavallée, along with several journalistic supporters, had fashioned to win political approval for his dream of a national conservatory. *Jeanne d'Arc* had been a big success in Montreal, but no one of influence in Quebec City, the provincial capital, had seen it. So *La dame blanche* was brought to Quebec, at considerable expense, specifically to attract an audience of influential opinion leaders and lawmakers.

But none came.

None came because, exactly at this moment in Quebec politics, a crisis was being played out, consuming the attention of every politician and every newspaper commentator in the province. Lavallée's timing couldn't have been worse. In March, just as Lavallée was preparing *La dame blanche*, the Liberal lieutenant-governor of Quebec had fired the Conservative premier, and in the resulting chaos an election was called for just before the show was scheduled to open—the week before. Worse, the election itself was a virtual tie, so for weeks afterward Quebec politicians were involved in a drama of their own, trying to figure out who should form the government. The new premier, Henri-Gustave Joly, finally managed to cobble together a plan that would keep him in government, but the politicians whom Lavallée was trying to influence with *La dame blanche* were exhausted by the election campaign and obsessed with the aftermath. The creation of a national music conservatory was very likely the last thing on their minds.

Nonetheless, just six weeks later, in the middle of June 1878—in exactly the same crisis-laden political climate as had prevailed in

May, but now aggravated further by a provincial strike—Lavallée tried again and formally proposed his conservatory project. He must have felt that on the heels of the twin successes of *Jeanne d'Arc* and *La dame blanche*, it was now or never to push ahead, although it didn't take a political genius to realize that the likelihood of his proposal being accepted was slim to nonexistent. Premier Joly and his cabinet simply had too many other pressing items on their agenda—most importantly, keeping themselves politically alive. The petition did work its way through various parliamentary committees, but it was formally declined in the fall of 1878 on procedural grounds. While the political upheaval of the time undoubtedly contributed to the decision, it seems clear that Lavallée and his artistic ambitions were at odds with the prevailing mentality of the ruling powers in Quebec society. But Lavallée was not to be deterred easily. The dreams he had formed in Paris of music in the service of national goals were very powerful—and he had formed them relatively late in his life. He was now in his thirties and, in effect, was just beginning his real musical career. Time was not on his side.

But fate intervened. Just as Lavallée was swallowing his disappointment at the legislative failure of his conservatory project, a major commission came his way. In the fall of 1878, Canada was to receive a new Governor General to replace Lord Dufferin, who had served in the post for six years. His replacement would be John Campbell, Marquess of Lorne, a statesman, writer, and, perhaps most importantly, the husband of Princess Louise, the fourth daughter of Queen Victoria. (Lake Louise is named after her.) To mark the arrival in Canada of Lord Lorne and Princess Louise, the Quebec government commissioned Lavallée and poet Napoléon Legendre to create a major cantata to be performed in their presence. The cantata would be one of the largest and most significant compositions of Lavallée's entire career, an ambiguous and somewhat cynical vote of confidence offered him by the government that had just turned down his beloved conservatory project.

Lord Lorne and Princess Louise were due in Quebec in November, so in late August Lavallée began work in furious haste. The cantata was designed to be a semi-religious work in seven movements, performed by a chorus of 150 voices and an enormous orchestra, with solos, duets, and obbligatos from a group of four featured singers—a Handel-style oratorio, a *Messiah* for the New World. After paeans to the geography and land of Quebec and a salute to the viceregal couple, the highlight of the piece was to be the finale, in which Lavallée cleverly set "God Save the Queen," "Vive la Canadienne," and "Comin' thro' the Rye" (a nod to Campbell's Scottish roots) to play simultaneously in a riot of musical inspiration and cross-cultural accommodation.

As it turned out, Lorne delayed his visit to Quebec until June of 1879, at which point he took up his summer residence in Quebec's famed citadel (a tradition started by his predecessor, Lord Dufferin). Lavallée, assuming a fall performance, had already long finished writing the cantata, so in April he set about preparing the forces to perform it—an immense choir, a large orchestra, and four soloists carefully selected to include two francophone and two anglophone singers. The cantata was on a significantly different order of complexity than either of the two operas that Lavallée had produced in the two previous years. It was a brand-new composition, having its world premiere for an ultra-distinguished audience in a province in political turmoil—and thus it was both politically sensitive and musically ambitious. In every aspect of the production, the stakes were enormously high.

It was not lost on Lavallée or his supporters that the government and the ecclesiastical powers of Quebec were more than happy to make use of his talents when it suited their purposes, but saw no need to provide him any recompense when it came to acceding to his desire for his conservatory. Power often uses art in this way, so perhaps the exploitative treatment of Lavallée is not as surprising as it might be. As we shall see, the relationship between the government and Lavallée only deteriorated further when a controversy erupted about who should pay for the expenses incurred in the creation of the cantata.

The big evening was on June 11, 1879. The venue was Quebec City's brand-new skating rink (the same place where, a year later, "O Canada" would be first performed), chosen because it could accommodate 1,500 people. Quebec's elite was in attendance— and the response to the work was rapturous. Every review noted the excellence of the orchestra and the chorus, the skilled conducting of Lavallée, the charm of the various soloists, and the perfection of the score. The finale with three tunes playing together was a complete sensation. After the performance, Lavallée was called over to the viceregal box for congratulations. Princess Louise seemed truly touched by the composition. The Governor General, by comparison, only sent Lavallée a cool note in the mail thanking him for his efforts. But the evening succeeded beyond the most extreme expectations of its sponsors.

The cantata should have, or could have, been a turning point in the musical history of Quebec, its coming of age. But its success was not enough to move the authorities of the province to rethink their position on a national conservatory, or even to offer Lavallée some official position. Or anything else. Lavallée had done what they needed done, and that was that. Lavallée's friend, the critic Joseph Marmette, exploded in anger in the pages of *La minerve*:

The king of the evening, M. Lavallée, has just pulled off the greatest musical event that's ever been presented in this country and that with a success that won him our ovations and warmest thanks. We have among us a great artist, a master. But what sort of life have we left him? What mark of sympathy and encouragement are we going to give him? Are we going to let him waste his talent and his life forever giving piano lessons so he and his family won't starve?

Lavallée's frustration over the fruitlessness of his campaign despite the success of the cantata was exacerbated by the fact that he found himself personally on the hook for many of the expenses incurred in mounting the event. Lavallée had been given a budget for it, but he had spent more than allotted to ensure the very best performance possible, adding extra rehearsals, bringing in soloists from abroad, and attending to every detail. Depending on whose account you read (and how sympathetic they were to the composer), Lavallée either was told to go ahead and spare no cost by his government commissioners or else he wilfully spent more money than he had out of sheer impudence or negligence. But in either case, it should have been irrelevant. Even if he had managed the expenses poorly, one would have thought that, given the success of the performance and the political importance of that success, someone would have found a way to reimburse the one person most responsible for it.

No one did, and the debts that Lavallée incurred over the cantata performance hung over him for many years. It seems a cruel injustice. It may be that Lavallée was a victim of the confusing and changing political situation in Quebec at the time. When the cantata had been presented in June, Luc Letellier de St. Just had been the lieutenant-governor of Quebec and Henri-Gustave Joly the premier. By October, they were both gone, Letellier having been fired by John A. Macdonald and Joly succeeded as premier by Joseph-Adolphe Chapleau. So both the chief politicians who had commissioned the cantata from Lavallée were now history, and their opponents were in power. Maybe they denied Lavallée's claims out of spite; maybe the claims just got lost in the government shuffle.

It should also be noted that Calixa Lavallée had enemies within the musical establishment of Quebec. Lavallée's insistence on a professionalized, authoritative school of musical instruction raised the hackles of the amateur, poorly trained, occasional music teachers in the province; they were convinced that higher professional standards might put them out of business. This may not seem like a very potent lobbying force, but music teachers in every part of the province allied with each other did have a certain political clout. Lavallée would face exactly the same sort of opposition in the United States half a decade later while attempting to professionalize American musical education. It's impossible to make any change in a complex society without disenfranchising someone—and those about to be disenfranchised seldom accept that change without a fight.

Whatever the reasons, what should have been Lavallée's greatest triumph on his return to Quebec, the Lorne cantata, turned into one of his biggest nightmares. Exhausted from the work of both composition and performance, saddled with debts of which no one would relieve him, and no closer to his cherished conservatory project, Lavallée entered 1880, just after his thirty-seventh birthday, ill and dispirited.

What he could not know in that January was that the events of the next six months would cement his reputation forever. They were the months that would bring him eternal national and international fame—the months that produced his three-minute gift to his nation, its national anthem.

EIGHT

THERE MAY HAVE BEEN a reason that Governor General
Lorne was so cool to Calixa Lavallée after the performance
of the cantata in Lorne's honour, when everyone else—including Princess Louise, the press, and the government—was so
enthusiastic.

At the very moment that the strains of the cantata were being
heard in the Quebec City skating rink, Lorne had in his desk
drawer a poem that he himself had written, "Dominion Hymn,"
which he was mulling over as the text for a potential national
anthem for the fledgling country of which he was now the viceregal head. He believed it was time, twelve years after its creation,
for Canada to establish its own national symbols. And a national
anthem was near the top of that list.

He felt he could ably supply the lyrics to such an anthem. He
was a successful writer, after all. And he had a composer in mind
to write the music—but it wasn't Calixa Lavallée, who may otherwise have seemed a logical choice right at that moment. Lorne had
bigger fish to fry.

He wanted Canada's national anthem to be written by Sir
Arthur Sullivan, then at the height of his fame along with his

partner William S. Gilbert. *The Pirates of Penzance* had just opened in London; *H.M.S. Pinafore* was still fresh in the public's mind. Gilbert and Sullivan were world-famous.

And, remarkably, Sullivan complied. I guess it's hard to say no when the queen's son-in-law asks you to write the national anthem for an entire country, and so it was that Sullivan's "Dominion Hymn" was written while he was a guest of Lord Lorne and Princess Louise at Rideau Hall in March of 1880. It's one of the more obscure works of the great English composer, if not his most obscure. Not one Canadian in a million knows that Arthur Sullivan wrote a national anthem for Canada.

And that's because it's terrible. Governor General Lorne might have been able to wield enough influence to get Sullivan to write a national anthem for Canada, but he didn't have enough influence to make sure it was any good. The music for "Dominion Hymn" is insipid and uninspired. If Sullivan spent more than twenty minutes on the piece, it would be a surprise. He certainly wouldn't have been tremendously moved by Lorne's lyrics—seven eight-line stanzas, each followed by the same chorus:

O bless our wide Dominion,
True freedom's finest scene;
Defend our people's union,
God save our Empire's Queen.

Hard to imagine that those sentiments were going to serve the new Dominion, in all its political complexity, especially well, even if Sullivan had written something other than his pedestrian, forgettable tune.

"Dominion Hymn" was performed twice: once in Ottawa in March of 1880, soon after it was written, and again in May by an orchestra in Montreal for a blue-ribbon audience. The hymn, for all its failings, might well have supplanted "God Save the Queen" as Canada's national anthem; it obviously had powerful backing and interests in its favour.

But it takes more than subtle maneuvering and political clout to make a national anthem successful. It takes a composition with an indefinable, mysterious quality in its music and words that captures the hearts and imaginations of a people. In 1880 there were many who felt, as Governor General Lorne did, that the new nation of Canada needed such a song. Confederation had accomplished many prosaic political, military, and economic ends in 1867, but it had also raised the possibility of creating a new nationality altogether. Symbols were needed to express this new nationality— to solidify its place on the continent and in the world. For most English-speaking Canadians, their nation and its symbols needed to have some connection to the imperial centre of Great Britain, but they needed to reflect Canadian individuality as well. It's a complex and intricate dance—one that we've been attempting to perform one way or another for a century and a half.

Outside of Sullivan's "Dominion Hymn," there were other candidates for Canada's national anthem in English Canada. Chief among these was "The Maple Leaf Forever," written by a Toronto schoolteacher, Alexander Muir, to celebrate Confederation in 1867. "The Maple Leaf Forever" is a quirky sort of tune, but not without its charms, and despite its frankly militaristic tone ("In days of yore, from Britain's shore / Wolfe the dauntless hero came"), "The Maple Leaf Forever" had its champions in English Canada well into the mid-twentieth century.

Sullivan's "Dominion Hymn" itself was no mere novelty—it was obviously intended to be taken seriously. Its public performance at the beginning of a special Montreal Philharmonic concert on

May 27 was attended by the Governor General, along with Princess Louise and her brother, Prince Leopold. There can be little doubt that Lorne felt that his words and Sullivan's music made a potent combination. Luckily for Canada, Sullivan's music was so uninspired and pedantic that the "Dominion Hymn" was soon forgotten. Otherwise, our flag would be ascending to the rafters after another Olympic hockey gold medal with an arena full of ecstatic fans singing, "O bless our wide Dominion, true freedom's fairest scene; defend our people's union, God save our Empire's Queen!"

None of this maneuvering towards the creation of an imperialistic national hymn for the country sat well with the ultramontane, suspicious, conservative nationalist forces in Quebec. Even the more progressive Liberal party in the province was wary of this new Canadian identity, with its frank declarations of English domination and British imperialism—echoes of Lord Durham. The spectre of assimilation never leaves the French Canadian heart for long, and it was large and menacing in the years after Confederation, when the emphasis in the new Canada was on the emerging West rather than on the old, settled colonies of Upper and Lower Canada. A West, ironically, first explored and settled by French Canadians in the eighteenth century, but in which nineteenth-century French Canadians had almost no interest. English-Canadian nationalism was gaining strength daily in the 1870s. So it was felt that French-Canadian nationalism, its symbolic opposite, needed a powerful declaration as well. It's the iron law of Canadian politics, Newtonian in its inevitability: a strong action by one side of our cultural divide produces an equal and opposite reaction on the other. So the need for a reinvigorated statement of French-Canadian reality was in the air in Quebec as 1879 gave way to 1880.

In the Quebec of that time, the key institution around which the forces of Quebec nationalism rallied was the famous Société

Saint-Jean-Baptiste, still to this day the premier nationalistic force in the province. The society was first created by a journalist, Ludger Duvernay, in the mid-1830s, when Quebec pride and patriotism were first beginning to emerge. He originally named his association after a similar group that had been active in the French Revolution of 1830, Aide-Toi et le ciel t'aidera (God helps those who help themselves). Duvernay officially founded the group in March of 1834 but he wanted to create a special event at which to celebrate its goals and philosophy. He noted that the English merchants of Montreal had their own semi-secret and very powerful society, the Freemason Grand Lodge of Quebec. The Lodge met every year for a banquet on the twenty-fourth of June. As a mark of protest and mischievousness, Duvernay decided that his association would hold its annual banquet on the very same day. So on June 24, 1834, sixty members of the Aide-Toi association met in Montreal to drink to the health of "le feu sacré de l'amour de la patrie." George-Étienne Cartier, later a Father of Confederation, wrote a song for the occasion, "Ô Canada! Mon pays! Mes amours!," which for many decades was considered a possible candidate for a Quebec national song. Duvernay's association continued to meet annually, although their amiable get-togethers were interrupted by the Rebellions of 1837 and 1838. Duvernay himself was placed on a list of rebels to be arrested during the Rebellions, but he was warned in time and fled to New England, where he remained for five years. Returning to Quebec, he reorganized the Aide-Toi organization into something more substantial and long-lasting. And because its annual event was held on June 24, which was the feast day of St. John the Baptist in the Catholic world, he named his group La Société Saint-Jean-Baptiste. It retains the title to this day and is still one of the most powerful nationalist associations in Quebec and throughout French-speaking North America.

In 1874, to celebrate its fortieth anniversary, the Saint-Jean-Baptiste Society in Montreal had organized and hosted an immense gathering devoted to the contemporary meaning of French North America and the spiritual, political, and cultural impact of French-Canadian identity. With delegates from all over the continent, especially the northern United States, the conference was an immensely powerful affirmation of the French fact in North America, with flags, rallies, conferences, masses, marches, and celebrations galore. The event became a beachhead for a distinctively conservative French Canadian identity and nationalism, rooted in the past, in the Catholic faith, and in a vision of an ideal Quebec that was deeply at odds with the emerging industrial civilization of North America.

The success of the 1874 Montreal conference inspired the Quebec City chapter of the Saint-Jean-Baptiste Society to organize a similar international convention for 1880, to be held on and around Saint-Jean-Baptiste Day. This time it was for up to forty thousand delegates. And in keeping with the renewed interest in Quebec nationalism of the time, the organizers of the conference decided to use its prominence and significance to create and premiere a "national hymn" for Quebec, an anthem for French Canada. They wanted a special kind of song that would do what all national anthems do—celebrate and immortalize a people, a nationality, and a culture, and cement a political reality. A French political reality. And, of course, the name that this French political nation had had for centuries was *Canada*. The French Canadians were *Canadiens*. So it's no surprise that this French anthem would eventually be called "Ô Canada." No other name would make sense. From this seed our anthem eventually blossomed.

To get the anthem they were looking for, the organizers of the 1880 convention first floated the idea of holding an open competition for the song. However, they realized they didn't have enough time to do that successfully, so they created a twenty-three-person music committee to decide how to get the *chant national* written. It was chaired by a journalist and musician named Ernest Gagnon and included a leading conservative thinker and judge, Adolphe-Basile Routhier, and Calixa Lavallée among its members. But deliberations for expressly political songs are themselves intensely political, and by March of 1880, just three months before the anthem was due to be performed for the first time, the committee had made no progress.

So, without telling anybody, Gagnon, Routhier, and Lavallée decided to take matters into their own hands. They would write the anthem themselves, committee be damned. Gagnon got it organized: Routhier, an amateur poet, would supply the words; and Lavallée, of course, the music. Lavallée asked if he could write the music first, and Routhier agreed. After a few weeks of agonizing over the tune's melody, harmony, and structure, Lavallée was done. Gagnon invited Routhier over to Lavallée's house one afternoon to hear the finished product (a plaque still notes the residence, on Couillard Street in Quebec City), and that very night, in a burst of inspiration, Routhier composed all the words to the anthem, all four verses—lyrics that are still sung to this day, unchanged, throughout French Canada. Gagnon had suggested "Ô Canada! Pays de nos aïeux" (O Canada, country of our ancestors) to Routhier as a possible first line to the anthem; Routhier changed it slightly, to "terre de nos aïeux" (land of our ancestors), the word *terre* having a softer sound, and he finished it from there. "O Canada" had entered the world. To hide what they had done, Gagnon made up a little story, claiming that the lieutenant-governor of the province, Théodore Robitaille, had come across Routhier's verses and had begged Lavallée to set them to music. Robitaille, delighted to have an anthem, was happy to play along with this tiny charade. Nobody questioned the story, the anthem was delightedly accepted, and the piece was published in April of 1880. (Gagnon's bit of subterfuge was very successful—it's still routinely quoted today as the origin of the anthem.)

A lovely first-person account from the time gives us a sense of just how exciting this moment was for the participants, especially for Calixa Lavallée. J.K. Foran was a student at Laval University when Lavallée was working on his famous composition. Supposedly, Lavallée had tried out several versions of the tune for his friends before he settled on the finished product. And then, according to Foran,

> One night, there were six or seven of us in the room [at Laval]. Around nine o'clock Pierre Rouselle, the university secretary, and Trudel, the great tenor, burst into the room, with a small nervous man who was very excited. He clapped his hands together, and said, "I have it, I've finally found it, I've got it, come, listen." He moved to the piano. For a moment his hands seemed to be communicating an electric current to the piano. Then, throwing his head back, he played for the first time, his masterpiece: it was Calixa Lavallée, he was playing "O Canada." A few minutes later, Trudel sang us Routhier's words, accompanied by the very author of the hymn par excellence of Canada. I felt transported to Strasbourg, the night when Rouget de l'Isle played and sang "La Marseillaise" for the first time.

"O Canada" may not be quite on the level of "La Marseillaise," but Foran understood the potent symbolism that the anthem presented to its original audiences. Since those first moments of its creation, "O Canada" has inspired and energized hundreds of millions of people with a mysterious power that language can only hint at.

But the song did not just resonate because of its music—in addition to Lavallée's inspired tune, Routhier's original French lyrics were almost pitch-perfect. They created exactly the kind of anthem their sponsors hoped for. They were a statement of pride and a somewhat-defensive belligerency which was the essence of the ultramontane view of Quebec's place in the world. Even today, as old as they are, they sum up a good deal of the desires and hopes and fears and contradictions of the complicated reality of modern French Canada:

Ô Canada! Terre de nos aïeux,
Ton front est ceint de fleurons glorieux!
Car ton bras sait porter l'épée,
Il sait porter la croix!
Ton histoire est une épopée
Des plus brillants exploits.
Et ta valeur, de foi trempée,
Protégera nos foyers et nos droits.
Protégera nos foyers et nos droits.

Routhier was not a poet, but a judge. He was also a fiercely conservative voice in the politics of post-Confederation Quebec, as well as an ultramontane writer of considerable skill, often courting controversy for his deeply religious and anti-modern views. He made a strange artistic companion for the much more liberal Lavallée—but the intersection of art and politics that is needed to create a national hymn inevitably produces such contradictions and collaborations.

The frank conservatism and aggressive nationalism of the French words to "O Canada" often surprise English Canadians. They represent a right-wing view of the province that can offend the sensibilities of the more modern and secular Quebec of today (one of the reasons "O Canada" is now less popular in Quebec than it is in the rest of the country), but they still express a conception of the historical destiny of the people of French Canada that resonates in the heart of the province. "Ô Canada," the original French version, is not just a reflection of patriotism and pride; it is an explicit call to arms.

That historical view of a proud and embattled Quebec begins with the first line, "Ô Canada! Terre de nos aïeux." There could not be a more appropriate opening for a French Canadian national hymn in a province whose official motto became *Je me souviens*. "Terre de nos aïeux" (land of our ancestors) places the contemporary French Canadian in a perspective that stretches not forwards, but backwards. That puts the history and travails and pain of Quebec's past front and centre in the present-day consciousness of French Canadians. English Canada would never start an anthem by identifying the nation as the country of our ancestors—and not just because, for many of us, Canada was not in fact the country of our ancestors. It's more that English Canadians have consistently identified Canada with its future, not its past. Whether that was expressed in Sir John A. Macdonald's vision of a railway linking the country from sea to sea or Sir Wilfrid Laurier's invocation that "the twentieth century belongs to Canada," the future has always been the locus of English Canada's view of the country's glory.

But the past, the history of Quebec, is the locus of glory imagined by Routhier and "Ô Canada." "Ton front est ceint," the next line reads, "de fleurons glorieux" (Your brow is garlanded with glorious flowers). A hint of Greek and Roman majesty here surrounding the figure of Canada, of Quebec—a hero's aura.

Routhier, as we have seen, fit his lyrics to Lavallée's music when he wrote the words for "O Canada," and he has caught a change in the musical mood of the anthem after the first two lines, when the piece subtly turns from a hymn to a march. (This is the section that in English begins, "With glowing hearts we see thee rise.") Routhier matches Lavallée's subtle militarism, with its insistent bass drumbeat, in his lyrics, and writes, "Car ton bras sait porter l'épée, / Il sait porter la croix!" (Because your arm knows how to carry the sword, it knows how to carry the cross). Words that always shock English Canadians when they first come across them, and even surprise contemporary French Canadians. This ultra-explicit identification of Quebec with the Catholic faith, and with a strident, belligerent faith at that, is the essence of the ideology which ruled Quebec at the time. The sword joined with the cross, the comforts of religion flowing out of the aggressiveness of combat, the absolute indivisibility of the nation and the Church—that's "O Canada" in French. This is followed by a declaration of a sort of defensive pride: "Ton histoire est une épopée / Des plus brillants exploits" (Your history is an epic of brilliant deeds).

And finally, the French version of "O Canada" closes with a powerfully stated declaration of Quebec's instinct for survival: "Et ta valeur, de foi trempée, / Protégera nos foyers et nos droits" (And your valour, steeped in faith, will protect our homes and our rights). "O Canada," in the original, ends in a deeply political, almost confrontational spirit of *la survivance*. A more perfect summation of the value system of late nineteenth-century Quebec can hardly be found—this odd amalgam of pride and despair, glory and defensiveness. We in English Canada, singing about our home and native land, and glowing hearts and the True North strong and free, completely miss the emotional power of the French version of the anthem. Our Canada is cheerful and open, even as we stand on guard for it. The Canada of the French version, which exists to protect our homes and our rights, may be glorious, but it is not looking eagerly to the future. It is suspicious but defiant, determined to harness the brute power of history and faith to achieve eventual spiritual victory. That's what French audiences hear today, even as they consider the sentiments of the anthem old-fashioned and remote. But they were not remote to the audiences who heard the anthem in 1880; they were a battle cry.

...

The words and music to "O Canada" were most likely finished by early April of 1880, and they were published later in the month, ahead of the massive late-June French Canadian national convention for which the piece had been written. The anthem's first public performance was planned for the afternoon of June 24, Saint-Jean-Baptiste Day, as part of a giant open-air Mass that was to be given by Archbishop Elzéar-Alexandre Tascherean on the Plains of Abraham. The Mass was to be a monstrous event, with Taschereau assisted by five hundred priests in front of an audience of over forty thousand people. It was meant to be inspiring and dramatic, a visual and spiritual declaration of the strength of the French fact in North America. "God Save the Queen" was to be played just after the Mass, to recognize the presence of Governor General Lorne. But the unveiling of "O Canada" was scheduled for the very end of the afternoon—pride of place for its first-ever public performance.

It never happened.

For some reason never explained, "O Canada" was removed from the program at the last minute and not presented on the Plains of Abraham that afternoon as planned. No one knows why. Maybe it was considered bad form to upstage "God Save the Queen," especially with the Governor General present. Maybe the Church objected. We shall likely never know. But it is a shame that "O Canada" was denied its scheduled, momentous, premiere. Few other anthems would have had such a showy, theatrical beginning.

However, "O Canada" did get its premiere that evening, in an instrumental version only, at a banquet given for up to eight hundred special guests representing the cream of the crop of Quebec society. It took place in the same Quebec City skating rink where Lavallée's cantata for Governor General Lorne had been presented almost exactly a year earlier. A selection of brass bands from both Canada and the United States played the brand-new anthem, to a tremendous response. The next day the piece was heard again, this time by an audience of about six thousand, at an afternoon concert given at the home of the lieutenant-governor. Bleachers had been set up for the occasion. A fine morning had given way to scudding clouds and threats of rain in the afternoon. Just as "O Canada" began, peals of thunder boomed in the afternoon sky. Despite the weather, another success.

The first time Adolphe-Basile Routhier's words to "O Canada" were heard along with the music was on June 27, three days after the orchestral premiere, during a Mass held at Saint-Jean-Baptiste Church. Again, the anthem made a powerful first impression. It's interesting to note how often the early performances of "O Canada" were tied up with religious festivities or ceremonies. The "national song," as it was called, was really a national hymn, a quasi-religious invocation of the spirit of Quebec and French Canada. In Quebec, the needs of the state, the people, the Catholic Church, and the land itself have always been twisted into one complex tissue of emotion. And "O Canada" spoke to it all.

It would be satisfying to be able to say that once "O Canada" had been brought into the world, it was an immediate hit and won instant and lasting acclaim. But it wasn't, and it didn't. After its portentous debuts in June of 1880, it virtually disappeared in Quebec for almost twenty years. Calixa Lavallée had been dead for close to a decade before "O Canada" began its ascent into our consciousness, in both French and English Canada, as the song of our nation. For Lavallée, "O Canada" had been the intense work of a few weeks, maybe a few months, but then abandoned. In his mind, it would not have ranked in significance anywhere near the Lorne cantata, or even the productions of *Jeanne d'Arc* or *La dame blanche*. It was a piece written for a momentous occasion, and then forgotten.

It certainly did not change or arrest in any way Lavallée's continuing deteriorating relationship with his home province. Instead of being the beginning of a new chapter for Lavallée, "O Canada" was actually the end of one. On one of the few occasions the piece was performed after its premiere—on November 22, 1880, five months later, in a Quebec church—Calixa Lavallée was no longer in Canada to hear it.

Sometime in September, just a few weeks after the premiere of his masterpiece, Calixa Lavallée left Quebec for the United States once again. This time, he never returned. Between the gossip, the small-mindedness, and the lack of respect he had received from the general public—added to the indifference the government had shown about his conservatory project—Lavallée had had enough. He decided once and for all to exile himself from his home country. For the last eleven years of his life, until his death in 1891, he lived in Boston, returning only once for a visit of but a few days. Lavallée and Quebec had parted company for good. "O Canada" was his swan song.

Lavallée's abrupt departure from his home province has fuelled many romantic myths about the scorned artist who was too sophisticated to be appreciated by the philistines at home, which has situated Lavallée in the company of Dante, Mozart, James Joyce, and many others. In truth, Lavallée had always had one foot and one part of his heart in the United States. He had been an American minstrel, an American soldier, an American composer. His wife was American; so were many of his friends. He was now approaching thirty-eight. He had lived in Canada for only seven of the previous twenty-two years. The United States had always been his second home, if not his first. His return there was part of a longstanding pattern.

Nevertheless, Lavallée left Quebec in the fall of 1880 a disillusioned man. Still carrying the debts from the Lorne cantata, no closer to his dreams of a national conservatory, he was tired of his meagre teaching income and his constant series of poorly attended concerts. These sentiments ring loud and clear in a letter Lavallée wrote to his friend Joseph Marmette in October of 1880, just after he left Quebec. Lavallée was in Hartford, at the home of an old friend, and in an expansive mood:

I am here like a grand lord at the home of my friend Duclos, an intelligent man, and very rich. His home is princely, horses at my disposal, a grand piano for working, and magnificent company, in sum, all that is required to spoil a man of my temperament. . . . When one returns here, one realizes the insignificance of the ideas of our poor country. I have travelled too much to stop and listen to the pretentious counsels that I could receive there.

And then Lavallée's tone changes, and he delivers, in effect, his own epitaph: "An artist is not meant to rot in an obscure place and especially not in an even more obscure country."

Lavallée had fled Quebec and Canada for good, in a bitter mood. But he had left behind something invaluable—two minutes of music that have come to define a nation.

NINE

W HAT IS IT ABOUT the music to "O Canada" that makes it so effective? How is it able to evoke tears, pride, a feeling of unity, a sense of country? Maybe it's just because it's a national anthem, and it borrows its emotional profile by sheer association: we play the anthem at certain times, the times are emotional, the song picks up the emotion of the occasion.

Perfectly reasonable, but almost assuredly wrong. Because by that theory any song would have the same effect if played at the same occasions—and every song does not. There is something deep in the musical tissue of "O Canada"—something in its DNA—that produces those effects, that makes it so powerful. Something hard to define, as music always is, but there nonetheless.

Music is mysterious. It's a process that starts with the very air around us moving in invisible patterns, triggering waves that enter our eardrums, which turn into a whirlwind of neurons and synapses and chemical reactions and electrical displacements more complex than any computer could hope to replicate. And which, most mysteriously of all, in the end result not in a simply physical process of soundwaves and vibrations and electrical currents but in emotion, spirit, and humanity. In sound.

What makes music especially interesting as it relates to human perception is how much information we process simultaneously when we listen to even the simplest work. At any given moment in a piece of music, our ears and brains and hearts are responding to a melodic pattern of notes, a rhythmic pattern of beats, a harmonic pattern of chords, an instrumental pattern of timbres, sometimes a literary pattern of words, and then a juxtaposed, interrelated pattern of words and music together. Music is the ultimate cognitive puzzle—it's not three-dimensional chess, it's more like twenty-dimensional chess. Which our brains can play effortlessly.

All of this makes analyzing music tricky. We never hear one aspect of music at a time; we hear everything all together all the time. But if we try, we can isolate various aspects of a musical piece that work on a subconscious level when we hear them together but can be observed independently if we take them apart.

So we can actually explain, to some extent, why "O Canada" works—why it has inspired so many soaring hearts, created so many catch-in-the-throat moments, rung the sounds of our country so successfully throughout the world.

The first thing we need to look at is the organization of the work. It's a tiny piece, but it's very cleverly put together. Of course, because "O Canada" is so familiar, we never really think about it beyond mumbling its words in some auditorium, or quietly humming its tune. But the structure of the song is significant because it provides the emotional arc on which the piece is built, and which our musical subconscious follows like a story in sound. More than anything else, that structure creates the potency of the anthem.

"O Canada" has three basic sections. The first begins with "O Canada! Our home and native land!" The middle section, which has a different feel to it, begins with the words "With glowing hearts we see thee rise." And finally, there's the last triumphant section, an echo of the first, which starts with "God keep our land glorious and free!" What's fascinating about the song is how those three parts build on one another. We need all three to make a complete artistic and dramatic statement.

We never think about it, because usually a brass band is blaring it out inches from our eardrums, but that first section of "O Canada" is, or should be, somewhat quiet—like a hymn, soft and contemplative. We need a starting point for the anthem, and Lavallée clearly wanted his piece to open in a calm, declarative manner. It's always played too loudly, but the music that accompanies "O Canada! Our home and native land!" is a church-like invocation of the country itself. At "True patriot love, in all thy sons command" (or now, "in all of us command"), the music gets a bit more joyous, hinting at what's to come. But it's a serene opening, straightforward and simple—establishing, however, as we'll see in a moment, all sorts of rhythmic and melodic markers (of which we're unaware when we first hear them) that Lavallée will exploit before he's done. The first section is the calm before the little storm that Lavallée surrounds us with in the second part of the piece.

In the second section, which starts "With glowing hearts we see thee rise," we hear the mood change quite abruptly. The church-like setting of the opening gives way to the inexorable beat of a march and the increasing tension of conflict. It's not surprising if you've never noticed this before, because this section is almost always played incorrectly: sweetly and softly. But if you listen attentively, you can hear that martial beat in the background. There's a sense of increasing drive and power that characterizes this section. And there's no doubt this was Lavallée's goal. If you look at the original sheet music of "O Canada," which reproduces the song exactly the way Lavallée wrote it, you can see in an instant that Lavallée wanted that martial beat front and centre. He wanted you to hear it very explicitly. The second section should be a power-ful and menacing bit of music.

The key to this is the music for the left hand of the piano accompaniment that Lavallée wrote for this section. It's a series of repeated octaves on a single note—a low D—that pound out insis-tently and incessantly, over and over again, never varying—*boom, boom, boom, boom*—like a fevered dream. Maybe Lavallée was remembering the sounds of his Civil War days, hearing the drum-beat that led men to battle, to glory, to the edge of heroism and death—it is the unmistakable sound of rising tension. We seldom, if ever, hear the original piano version of "O Canada" performed today, so we miss this abrupt change in mood of the piece. If you try and sing, "With glowing hearts we see thee rise, / The True North strong and free! / From far and wide, O Canada, we / stand on guard for thee," and imagine your left hand just playing one unchanging note over and over again as accompaniment, you'll see how obsessive, almost hysterical, it is. This was Lavallée's goal—he wanted to plunge us from the sweet, almost divine nature of the first part into the confused and inspiring anxiety of the second, into the dark reality of the world.

And it's interesting that when Adolphe Routhier first heard Lavallée play the piece, he picked up instantly on the emotions and spirit Lavallée wrote into this martial-sounding second sec-tion. It was this music, with its insistent drumbeat/heartbeat, that led Routhier to write the aggressive third line of the French ver-sion of the anthem: "Car ton bras sait porter l'épée, / Il sait porter la croix!" (Because your arm knows how to carry the sword, it knows how to carry the cross). Canada has moved from the bucolic "terre de nos aïeux" or "home and native land" of the first section to a threatening, sword-carrying nation in the second. Even Robert Stanley Weir, the author of the English lyrics, pays homage to the military sound of this section: this is where we start standing on guard for Canada, where our true patriot love morphs into something more combative. This sentiment appeared in the music before any lyrics were written. (And it's why not just any lyrics will do for a given piece of music; the words must respect the emotions hidden in the tones themselves.)

This powerful second section gives way to a third in which Lavallée cleverly joins together the emotions and spiritual meaning of the first two parts. It's a return to the opening, in a way—the music for "God keep our land" is exactly the same, note for note, as the opening "O Canada!" But now the music has taken on the intensity of that march-like second part. Hymn and march have coalesced.

You can tell because of the rhythmic profile of that third section. It's designed to ramp up the emotions. In the opening section, the phrase "O Canada," with its long—long—short—long rhythm ("Ohhhh—Caaaa—na—daaaa"), is immediately followed by another, smoother rhythm, on the words "our home and native land." The syncopated power of the first bit is calmed by the regularity of the next. But in the third section, that powerful opening rhythm keeps repeating, with no calming influences: first on "God keep our land," then immediately on "glorious and free," and finally on the triumphant "O Canada" that leads to us standing "on guard for thee," an "O Canada" which is repeated as we reach the climax of the piece. In music, this foreshortening, this accelerating of phrases, is often used to ramp up the emotional impact of a work. Lavallée has used the technique brilliantly to bring "O Canada" to a powerful close, on virtually the highest note of the piece.

A hymn that turns into a march that turns into a hymn and march together—this shape-shifting nature is a key secret of our anthem: why it works, why it inspires, why it thrills. It takes us on a dramatic and emotional journey, from the simplicity of the opening to the anxiousness of the middle section to the apotheosis of the ending. It has a shape, a meaning, and listeners have been responding to that shape for a century and more, even if they're not aware they're doing so.

But there's more to the anthem than just its structure. There are many subtle tricks hidden in the piece to reinforce its three-act configuration and to give it musical unity. The chief one is the use of the simple little rhythm that we hear right at the beginning of the piece, the rhythm that accompanies the words "O Canada" and more specifically *Canada*. Without realizing it, we hear echoes of that word throughout the entire work, even when the word itself isn't there.

Here's how Lavallée pulls that off. Listen to the rhythm that he uses for the word *Canada* right at the beginning. It's long—short—long, *Caa-na-daa*. Tap the rhythm of those syllables on the table beside you as you sing it. And then notice how many other times that *Caa-na-daa* rhythm shows up in the piece. It's there, sometimes obviously, sometimes disguised, over and over again. It is a subliminal template that runs through the whole composition so that, unconsciously, we're hearing *Canada* (or the rhythm of it) again and again as we listen. It's in those tiny little syllables that "O Canada" begins its journey to inspiration and meaning.

The first time you hear it, of course, is right at the beginning of the piece, where *Caa-na-daa* is proceeded by a long *Ohhh*, so that the rhythm is actually long—long—short—long. That exact same rhythm is repeated in the very next line of the piece: "true patriot love" has exactly the same rhythm as "O Canada," long—long—short—long. *True pa-triot love. O Caa-na-daa.*

Why does Lavallée do this? Because our aural memories in music are not very good. To remember something, we need to hear it again and again. Otherwise, what should sound like music will instead sound confused and chaotic. Repetition, obvious or disguised, is the key to just about every successful piece of music ever written. It helps us to understand what we're listening to, to feel the patterns of the music, to make sense of it.

The two repetitions of that opening rhythm ("O Canada" and "true patriot love") are part of the hymn-like serenity of the first section of the piece. So when we move to the march-like middle section, we might expect to hear a different rhythm. Here's where Calixa Lavallée is so clever, and why he's something other than a run-of-the-mill composer.

Even though the emotional temperature of the middle section is quite different, that *Caa-na-daa* rhythm never disappears. "Glow-ing hearts" has the same rhythm as *Caa-na-daa*. So does "see thee rise"; so does "far and wide." They're identical, as is the next "O Canada," the one before "we stand on guard for thee." It's a very effective subliminal trick. On the one hand, this middle section has a different emotional feel to it, so our brains and hearts register it as a change, as the next step in a musical plot. On the other hand, there are many rhythmic ties back to that first section. These help remind us that we're still listening to the same piece we started with. Lavallée has reached musical nirvana, establishing difference and similarity, movement and comfort, change and stability, all at the same time.

That rhythmic unity continues into the last section. "God keep our land" has the same rhythm as the opening "O Canada"; so do "glorious and free" and the repeated "O Canada." In a piece of just over two minutes, we hear that opening *Ohhh Caa-na-daa* rhythm ten times, yet we hardly realize it. This is the mark of a skilful composer, creating unity for the listener without bringing attention to that fact.

There are other subtle compositional devices scattered throughout "O Canada," that make it so effective, starting with the tune itself.

We humans are very simple musical creatures, especially when it comes to melody—the part of the song we sing, the most visceral and psychologically complex part of any musical work. When a melody goes up, we feel elated, positive; when it goes down, we feel sad and disheartened. A great composer plays with those melodic directions just like a great playwright does—creating contrast and drama and emotional satisfaction over the course of a piece of music using only the contours of its melodic lines.

You would expect the melody of a national anthem, which is designed to inspire, to soar up at its beginning. Hum "The Star-Spangled Banner" to see for yourself. After a little downward motion on "Oh," the melody accompanying "say can you see" is a triumphant upward sweep of song, setting the tone of America within just a few seconds.

"O Canada" is different.

The primary direction of the melody at the outset of "O Canada" is downwards. When we sing "O Canada!" right at the beginning of the piece, there's a big descent (of five notes) between the na and da of Canada. A typically Canadian gesture, one might say: an expression of sadness, a hint of melancholy. It's like a musical sigh—a moment of defeat, a temporary holdup, a turning away from glory—just as we begin. Remember that "O Canada" was originally intended as the anthem of French Canada only—that early hint of sadness, a cloud masking the sun, makes real emotional and narrative sense for a nation believing itself oppressed, fighting for its survival. There's even a minor, melancholy chord in the harmony on which the last syllable of Canada is sung—a very unusual occurrence in what should be a powerful, optimistic statement of a nation's confidence.

But Lavallée reverses course in the next phrase of the piece. After the downturn at the beginning, up rises the melody, and our spirits, on "our home and native land." Although there's a hint of the opening melancholy on the falling interval between -*tive* and *land*, the mood is beginning to be more upbeat, more positive.

And the music continues inexorably upward in the next phrase, bundling up our emotions with it. "True patriot love in all thy sons command" (or now, "in all of us command") is almost completely ascendant in its motion, moving the melody higher and higher. The melancholy of the opening continues to give way to a more optimistic and positive feeling.

Next comes the march-like second section, and there is genius in its melodic line just as there is in its accompaniment. Listen to the rising and falling sections of melody Lavallée has created for this section, one of the most original features of the piece—they're like sheaves of wheat ruffling in the prairie sun, or waves lapping at the Atlantic shore. A teasing sort of melody, going up but then retreating, time and again. On "with glowing hearts," the melody goes up and down; it tries again to escape in "we see thee rise," then settles down for "the True North strong and free." And then, remarkably, the melody repeats itself, with "from far and wide" and "O Canada," before a powerful statement on "we stand on guard for thee." It's an amazing melodic section—the anthem stalls here, with the music going neither up nor down, just rolling over again and again, awaiting, expecting, building quite a bit of tension for such a small piece. With this tension in the melody accompanied by that pounding, drum-like left hand, sounding out the apocalypse, the emotional buildup here is quite powerful.

And then, in the third section of the piece, that tension is unleashed and the anthem reaches its powerful conclusion. How? By constantly rising and rising and rising until it reaches its highest note on the final *Canada*. It starts with "God keep our land," moving up a note for "glorious and free," then up again for "O Canada, we stand on guard for thee." Then, the big climax, saved until the very end—the last "O Canada, we stand on guard for thee"—with the highest note on *Canada*. You can see here why Routhier's French lyrics are so successful: unlike Weir, who merely repeats the "stand on guard" sentiment at the end of the piece, Routhier saves his most powerful lyric, the place to which the piece has been heading from the first line—"protégera nos foyers et nos droits" (will protect our homes and our rights)—for the musical climax.

In all respects—in form, rhythm, and melodic line—it's a very satisfying emotional journey. The piece may be short, but it has a musical narrative, a little story told in sound, with moments of reflection, triumph, sadness, ecstasy. The fact that it works on us more or less unconsciously doesn't take anything away from its structural, melodic, or rhythmic complexity. There's a great deal of method in its seeming spontaneity. Lavallée has created a minor masterpiece with his anthem, which accounts for its persistence and popularity.

One question remains: Did he do it alone? Did he write the music to "O Canada" all by himself?

It may seem like a strange question because we know the story of the song's composition, but a controversy has dogged the piece ever since it was first performed. The song's opening notes, its first few moments, sound almost exactly like the opening of a piece by Wolfgang Amadeus Mozart, "March of the Priests," which begins Act Two of his famous opera *The Magic Flute*. And when we say "almost exactly like," we're being kind. They're identical. They have the same rhythm, same melody, same tempo, same mood, and—most strikingly from a musical point of view—the same harmony. Remember, there's a minor chord on the *da* of "O Canada!" at the beginning of the piece, unusual for what should be an uplifting anthem. The Mozart march has exactly the same chord in exactly the same place. There are several different ways to harmonize the opening notes of "O Canada." Lavallée chose the least likely—but exactly the same one Mozart chose. If you didn't know better, for a moment you'd think you were listening to "O Canada" when you hear the opening to Act Two of *The Magic Flute*.

So did Calixa Lavallée plagiarize Mozart? *The Magic Flute* is one of Mozart's most famous operas, so there's little doubt that Lavallée would have known "March of the Priests." If the piece were more obscure, it would be easier to claim that the resemblance was just a coincidence. More likely, what happened was that Lavallée called upon the Mozart from his musical subconscious when he started to write "O Canada." Maybe he was mulling over the opening to the anthem, the intrinsic rhythm of the words "O Canada," and his subconscious made a connection between that rhythm and the opening of the Mozart march. It's more common in musical composition than we think. Famously, George Harrison's "My Sweet Lord" was shown to be an exact replica of an old girl-group song from the sixties, "He's So Fine," based on the same principle—his musical unconscious rewrote the original song without him being aware of it.

In the case of "O Canada" and "March of the Priests," though, the two pieces take off on distinctive musical and dramatic trajectories soon after those opening few seconds. There are similarities between the two works after the opening, but they are very subtle. It's really just the openings of the two works that sound so much alike. And that's not enough to prove that Lavallée stole the anthem from Mozart. He didn't—the greatness of "O Canada" belongs entirely to Calixa Lavallée. A lifetime of music, of playing and hearing and composing it, allied with an important and uplifting pursuit—the creation of a *chant national* for a nation dear to his heart—pulled from his creative spirit a minor masterpiece, two minutes of music that have moved seven generations of Canadians to hear in its tones a reflection of themselves. Music has this power, unique among the arts—to establish a visceral, spontaneous connection between people simply via movements of soundwaves as they float through the air, lodge in our consciousness, and transform ever after into emotional meaning.

TEN

IN A MORE PERFECT WORLD, or if life resembled a Hollywood screenplay, the composition of "O Canada" would have been Calixa Lavallée's finest moment. He would have been hailed as a national hero, been granted his wish for a national conservatory, and settled down in Montreal for many more years of highly productive activity.

As it was, "O Canada" was almost immediately forgotten after its first performances, Lavallée was left to fend for himself in a highly indifferent province, and finally, fed up with his situation in Quebec, he left Canada for Boston just months after the song was premiered, never to return.

Lavallée may have left Quebec in despair, but he recovered soon enough. He was immensely industrious in the last decade of his life, perhaps his most productive period ever. He did not spend his years in Boston in consternation and poverty. Rather, he enjoyed some of his most creative and satisfying years in New England.

Lavallée thrived in Boston primarily because that city provided him all the musical opportunities that Canada wouldn't, or couldn't. But the comfort he felt in New England was more complex than that. The region was also home to an immense and thriving francophone population—hundreds of thousands of Quebecers who had made their way south over the preceding forty years in search of employment in New England mill towns. Lavallée's wife's family had been part of that exodus. So Calixa Lavallée didn't feel himself in a completely foreign country when he was in the United States. In fact, all his life he saw in that country a more sympathetic home for French Canadians than in English Canada. In this he was an "annexationist," a believer in the political union of Quebec and America. And he was not alone in this belief— many of Quebec's most radical and most loyal sons and daughters shared it. The annexationist movement peaked during the debates around Confederation in the mid-1860s in Quebec, but it never entirely subsided. As for Lavallée, although he never wrote explicitly on any political subject, his belief in annexation seems to have been lifelong. It was common knowledge in the Boston of the 1880s that Lavallée felt a greater affinity with the United States, with its large French Canadian population, than he did with what he considered the radical Orange Order Protestant bigots of English Canada. *Musical Courier* magazine noted that the composer "always advocated the annexation of Canada to the United States and invariably urged French Canadians in New England to be loyal to their adopted country." The *Brooklyn Eagle* newspaper reported in the late 1880s that Lavallée had noted he was "proud to be American." In another interview, when asked about music education in the United States, he said, "We are a great people, and we need not feel astonished at any time what one of America's sons may have in store for us." Lavallée never lost his identity as a French Canadian, or wanted to. But his political and national loyalties were more fluid than could be contained in the tight boundaries of nationality as we understand them today. Those who wish to claim Calixa Lavallée as a great Canadian patriot or as a Quebec "national hero," as was common in the 1930s when conservative Quebec nationalism was at its height, are bound to be disappointed. Lavallée's connection to his homeland was never wavering, but it was also never simple-minded.

Professionally, Boston was everything Lavallée could have hoped for as a mature musician certain of his powers as a performer, conductor, composer, and educator. In the United States of the 1880s and 1890s, Boston may well have been the apex not only of musical life but of all American intellectual life. It was home to both Harvard University and the Massachusetts Institute of Technology. It was the centre of publishing in the United States; New York hadn't yet taken on that mantle. More importantly for Lavallée, at that time Boston was home to some of America's oldest and most prestigious musical institutions. The Handel and Haydn Society was America's oldest choral institution. The Boston Symphony Orchestra was founded in 1881, the year after Lavallée moved to the city (he performed with the orchestra in one of its earliest seasons). Half of the musical periodicals published in the United States were based in Boston. The city was also home to great musical education institutions, such as the New England Conservatory of Music, still in operation today, as well as major music publishers and instrument manufacturers. For a musician of Lavallée's talents and experiences, Boston was a mecca.

Lavallée seems to have been able to enter the thriving Boston musical scene rather effortlessly after his arrival there in late 1880. (He had, as usual, come alone—Josephine, Calixa Jr., and a second son, Raoul, not yet one at the time, remained in Quebec City.) Within a few months, he had begun teaching at Carlyle Petersilea's Music School, a major competitor to the New England Conservatory of Music; he had a demonstration contract with the Henry F. Miller Piano Company, which provided him with a studio in return for the use and endorsement of their instruments; and he was performing regularly in the Boston area. He was a successful and satisfied musician.

In addition to his burgeoning career as a performer and teacher, Lavallée redoubled his activity as a composer during his time in Boston. In his first few years in the city, he wrote and published two operas, the most significant pieces he was ever to compose. The two works are a sort of yin and yang in his career as a serious musician. The first of these, *The Widow / La veuve*, is a light opera in the nineteenth-century European tradition, a frothy, farcical story set to tuneful, ingratiating melodies which sometimes reach significant artistic heights. It was a big hit in late nineteenth-century America. The other opera, published but never produced, is the astonishing *TIQ [The Indian Question]: Settled at Last, A Melodramatic Musical Satire in Two Acts*—a Gilbert and Sullivan–style comic opera on native themes featuring Sitting Bull, Indian Commissioners, and Sioux Indians performing fake tribal dances while preparing to devour American settlers—a travesty of cultural insensitivity almost impossible to countenance. Minstrelsy for Indigenous, rather than black, Americans.

In both works, Lavallée showed himself to be very much a musician of his time, feeding public needs and responding to public tastes. *The Widow* was written to satisfy the late nineteenth-century desire for farce, tuneful music, and light entertainment. *TIQ*, for all the questionable nature of its cultural attitudes, was intended as a topical political satire—settling the West was a big issue, very much in the air in the United States in the 1880s. Lavallée's minstrel past had prepared him to write each opera. It had taught him the potential popularity of both sentimental farce and outrageous satire. Everybody was writing these kinds of pieces in Lavallée's day, even if they have fallen into almost complete neglect since—the tastes of late nineteenth-century America have not travelled well into the twenty-first. Still, although the most popular pieces of the time are now historical relics and curiosities, many of them were written with considerable skill.

As a composer in these now-forgotten genres, Lavallée crafted his works with uncommon skill, and he was extremely popular in his time. Certainly most of his work is derivative, based on styles and compositional forms borrowed from his contemporaries. But his larger works are professional and well-fabricated, even if they rarely push the boundaries of convention or taste. There were many other rival composers in North America during Lavallée's career, but not many who had emerged from the frontier backwardness of nineteenth-century Quebec. Given how undeveloped musical life was in the province at his birth, how little instruction he received, and how rudimentary the tastes of his Quebec audiences were, Lavallée's skills and accomplishments in the 1880s are nothing short of miraculous.

...

The Widow, perhaps Lavallée's most accessible work, seems to have been composed in Quebec in 1880 right before he left for the United States. That would place its gestation just after that of the cantata for the Governor General and pretty much coincident with "O Canada," in what was clearly a fertile period for Lavallée's compositional career. The libretto, attributed to one Frank H. Nelson, is loosely based on Voltaire's *Nanine*, which was itself inspired by Samuel Richardson's groundbreaking novel *Pamela*. It is a complicated and relatively nonsensical tale of romance, feuds, mistaken identities, and ultimately happy endings, which provided Lavallée and Nelson with many opportunities for musical and lyrical inspiration. The libretto was published in Boston in 1881, the score in 1882.

It was a considerable success, full of comic choruses and sentimental ballads, ensemble numbers and vehicles for its star performers. A travelling company called the Acme Opera Company added *The Widow* to its repertoire in the fall of 1881 and readied the piece for performance for its 1882 season. The premiere took place in Chicago in February of 1882, and the piece travelled for an entire season with the company to cities as far afield as Minneapolis, Baltimore, Washington, St. Louis, Cleveland, and New York. Reviews were mixed, not uncommon for the time, but the *Music Trade Review* of New York tried to put *The Widow* into a wider national context in its notice:

> A new opera, especially when composed by a musician living in this country . . . is received here with a prejudice which foreign operas are not subjected to. Mr. Calixa Lavallée, a Boston musician, has composed an opera called *The Widow* which has more musical value than the majority of light operas produced in this city during the last two decades, and the only reason that prevents it from becoming a success is the fact that he does not reside three thousand miles away from here.

In other words, if *The Widow* had been composed in Vienna or Prague, Americans would have loved it. Because it was composed in Boston, they weren't sure.

If *The Widow* fit very carefully into the conventions of English and French light opera of the time, *TIQ* is something else indeed. Political themes were a feature of both minstrelsy and serious opera in Lavallée's time, but it was Lavallée's minstrel experience that was obviously close at hand in the composition of this odd, virtually unimaginable Gilbert and Sullivan–meets–Sitting Bull satirical mash-up. Perhaps the fact that *TIQ* was much touted but never performed is a testament to the fact that even in its own time, it took satire and political theatre a step too far. But Gilbert and Sullivan were at their height when *TIQ* was written; their *Patience* had just opened, following the massive success of *The Pirates of Penzance*. Perhaps Lavallée was trying to import their successful formula in creating *TIQ*. No matter its origin, the fact that Lavallée wrote it in the first place makes clear that he was trying to be at the centre of musical theatre in the America of the 1880s—he was still after fame and fortune, still ambitious, still burning with musical desire. The move to Boston had not discouraged him but rather had fired his creative imagination, however questionable the results. And *TIQ*, as problematic as it is for a contemporary audience, is an accurate reflection of attitudes that prevailed throughout North America a century and a half ago.

Indigenous issues were politically front and centre when Lavallée began setting the *TIQ* libretto, by Will F. Sage and Phillips Hawley, in 1882. Sitting Bull of the Lakota Sioux had been a national figure in the United States since the Battle of the Little Bighorn in 1876. The Indian chief and holy man had just returned to the United States in 1881 after four years in Saskatchewan, where he had fled after his encounters with U.S. forces and General Custer. Although Sitting Bull surrendered to the U.S. government on his return, the Americans simply didn't know what to do with him. For the next several years, he would be held prisoner at one federal facility after another, without resolution of his fundamental claims or, alternately, prosecution for his supposed crimes. Sitting Bull's plunge into limbo after 1881 was symbolic of the turmoil and confusion surrounding the Americans' relationship with Indigenous peoples in the settlement of the West. While the relationship of the settler to Native Americans had been complex and nuanced in the eastern half of the continent, the situation in the West was more stark. The entire American enterprise in the mid- to late nineteenth century was focused on moving westward and taking possession of the abundant land and resources to be found there—in the way of which were Indigenous peoples with twenty-thousand-year-old claims on the territory and its riches. Conflict, bitter and genocidal, was inevitable.

It may be that Lavallée and his collaborators were merely naïve in thinking that the "Indian question" could be treated in a lighthearted way, through satire. Perhaps Lavallée failed to realize that the transgressive nature of the minstrel hall, where satire and comedy were permitted a sharp, ragged edge, didn't translate to the legitimate stage. Gilbert and Sullivan's whimsy did not travel especially well to an American context. Likely for a combination of these reasons, although the opera was completed in 1882, published in 1883, and optioned for performance by two separate companies, it was never produced.

TIQ was *The Mikado* using Indigenous American rather than Japanese stereotypes. And even though the lens of satire in the piece is focused almost entirely on the settling Americans rather than the honourable Sioux Nation, so much so that some critics have seen the opera as subversively pro-Indigenous, the result is hardly more bearable. At the opera's beginning, Sitting Bull and his warriors are coexisting peacefully with the soldiers sent to subdue them, going so far as to refuse weapons offered them. Soon, three female missionaries—Fitzgerald, Fitzgiggle, and Fitznoodle—arrive from Boston, more anxious to snare men than converts. Indian Commissioners also arrive on the scene determined to create trouble and eventually ply the Indians with alcohol, to the latter's inevitable, if temporary, ruin. However, in Act Two it is the Commissioners who are forced to plead for their lives. In the end, Sitting Bull's dignity and compassion prevail, and he orders the government officials off his land. But many remain, and the opera ends celebrating the joys of intermarriage as the Indian question is finally settled with romance and love. Throughout, Lavallée peppers the show with faux-Amerindian rhythms and textures, along with sentimental ballads for all the characters; the whole thing seems at times like a discarded alternative to the "Springtime for Hitler" number in Mel Brooks's *The Producers*.

Lavallée's foray into the world of opera in the United States, writing compositions at the highest level of musical competence and complexity, however they might have been received, revived in him his strongly held belief that homegrown North American composers needed to be afforded a great deal more respect and attention from North American audiences and critics than they were. In a series of articles he wrote for several Boston journals, Lavallée constantly emphasized the need for Americans to take their own creators and creative life seriously, to put away the inferiority complex that always situated artistic excellence—especially in classical music—elsewhere, namely in Europe. He had made exactly the same arguments in Montreal and Quebec City.

But in the United States, Lavallée was actually able to do something about the situation. He had finally found a place where his artistic visions and ambitions were not stunted by prejudice or indifference. By the last five or six years of his life, Lavallée had managed to launch two projects of the kind that had most inspired him when he was in Paris—creating a national school of composition and a national school of music education. It's just that the nation in question was not his own, but one he adopted and which adopted him—the United States. Calixa Lavallée became one of the most important figures in the history of American music.

...

The vehicle by which Lavallée accomplished these ends was an unexpected one. Lavallée had first attended a meeting of the Music Teachers National Association in the summer of 1883, two years after he relocated to Boston. It turned out to be one of the most fateful moments of his life. The MTNA was an organization lobbying for higher standards of instruction in American musical life. Lavallée had been interested in music education and the significance of music to the general spiritual health of a nation ever since his time in Paris in the mid-1870s. It was only natural that he would continue to pursue this aspect of his artistic life while in the United States. From his introduction to the organization that summer, the MTNA was to be the means by which Lavallée would make his most important cultural contributions to American music, contributions that would make him one of that country's most honoured educators and performers by the time of his death eight years later. He was to become "the Lafayette of our American musicians"— the foreign-born hero of a nation.

The defining moment of Lavallée's career as a champion of American music came in 1884, at that year's Music Teachers National Association annual convention in Cleveland. Serious American musical composition was still in its relative infancy in the 1880s, but Boston was a major centre of the emerging musical voice of the country. The Second New England School, as it has come to be called, consisted of a half dozen or so composers who, although still heavily influenced by European models, were beginning to create the outlines of a specifically American music. Needless to say, these American voices struggled to gain a hearing in the heavily Europeanized atmosphere of classical music in the United States in the 1880s and 1890s. Occasionally, a work of the group would be heard; most often their compositions were ignored or performed in small, obscure venues. The major orchestras and ensembles of the country just weren't interested. Between 1842 and 1880, for example, the New York Philharmonic performed 217 different works; just eight were by Americans.

Thus, it would have been incredibly daring at that time to suggest that a recital of all-American music be part of the Music Teachers National Association convention in Cleveland, with the cream of the crop of America's musical professionals present and the most critical ears in the country trained on the event. It would take nerve to suggest such a concert, determination to plan it, courage to perform it, panache to pull it off. Yet someone did it all—successfully.

Calixa Lavallée.

The concert took place on the afternoon of July 3, 1884. With Lavallée at the piano, a group of tough-minded teachers and critics assembled to hear something they had no idea was coming. Nineteen different works were on the program, by nineteen different composers—all American, a first in the history of the country. (Lavallée snuck in his own composition, "Le papillon," as an encore.) Most of the works were for solo piano, but Lavallée also included a string quartet, a piano trio, and a vocalist in the lineup. He had memorized the entire program, an accomplishment that would be long remembered.

Included in the performance were some composers about whom little is known—among them one woman, Luisa Cappiani—but the music of the men who were about to become known as the Second New England School was well represented. A gavotte by Arthur Foote opened the concert; a spring idyll by John Knowles Paine and a scherzino by George Whitefield Chadwick were also on the program. Most of these composers have fallen into obscurity today, but the real significance of the Cleveland concert was the important statement Lavallée was making to a major, high-profile musical audience. He was demonstrating that there were American composers of excellence whose work deserved the highest level of performance by seasoned professionals and more frequent presentation to domestic audiences. It was a challenge to both educators and musicians to shake off their long-held prejudice against native-born composers and to listen to their music with fresh ears. Despite being a concert presented to a professional association at ten o'clock on a Thursday morning, it was one of the boldest steps in the history of American music.

The 1884 concert shows all the dynamism of Calixa Lavallée wrapped up in one gesture—his confidence in his own programming and performing abilities, his fearlessness in the face of the unknown—and some of the sadness of the man as well. This is a concert that one assumes Lavallée would have preferred to have given in Montreal with a focus on Canadian composers, and in that vast gulf between what Lavallée was capable of providing to Quebec society and what that society was willing to accept falls a deep sense of the tragic. Lavallée offered himself to his native land and was met with derision and apathy, along with not-inconsiderable personal debts. So he took himself off to a second home—perhaps reluctantly, perhaps not—and became something of a national hero.

Lavallée's Cleveland concert was a major success. The *Cleveland Herald* reported that it was "one of the most interesting of many musical treats thus enjoyed by members of the association, namely, the recital of pianoforte compositions of native and resident composers, by Calixa Lavallée, of Boston, a most excellent pianist." The *Folio* noted that the concert created "a new departure in the musical history of this country." In the wake of the concert, the MTNA elected Lavallée vice-president for the state of Massachusetts. For the rest of his life, this organization became his most important professional connection, and through it he launched himself on a pioneering career as a leading spokesperson for the development and performance of American music.

Lavallée followed up his successful all-American recital in Cleveland with two similar concerts back home in Boston, in March of 1885. Both concerts were reviewed in the local press, and, for the first time, American compositions were given the sort of critical appraisal that had previously been reserved for imported classical music. Some of the reviews were positive, some not—but the very fact that classical reviewers were training their attention on American music was the point of the exercise, and an important breakthrough.

And it was one that got Lavallée noticed. His fame as a champion of American music began to spread, both in Boston and across the country. Both the *Folio* and *Musical Courier* featured him on their covers in the spring of 1885. That summer, the Music Teachers National Association followed up Lavallée's breakthrough piano recital of a year previous with an all-American orchestral concert, including a religious work by Lavallée himself, "Tu es Petrus." (To put this in perspective, it wasn't until January of 2017 that the Toronto Symphony Orchestra presented its first all-Canadian concert.) With his growing advocacy for American music, Lavallée became an increasingly active and respected member of the MTNA. The organization became a platform for him to advance his most radical and far-reaching ideas.

While his professional life seems to have been thriving in the early 1880s—with his connection to the MTNA, concerts with the new Boston Symphony Orchestra, and a host of teaching opportunities—his personal circumstances were at times troubled. Having left Josephine and the children at home in Quebec City, he had remained separated from his family for three years. But a tragedy reunited them. Calixa Jr., then fourteen, died suddenly in the spring of 1883, perhaps of appendicitis, and Josephine relocated to Boston soon after. Despite the melancholy circumstances that brought them back together, however, the Boston years were relatively prosperous and secure for the Lavallées, perhaps for the first time in their entire marriage.

It's likely that Josephine's presence also helped propel Lavallée into a position of authority and leadership within the expatriate French Canadian community in New England. The French Canadian populations of the state, both urban and rural, were healthy and active during Lavallée's time in Boston. Early in his stay, Lavallée became president of La Prévoyance, an immigrant settlement agency. In the fall of 1885, in the wake of the trial and execution of Louis Riel—an act which incensed francophones on both sides of the border—Lavallée organized a benefit concert for Riel's family in Fall River, Massachusetts, a textile-manufacturing town which, with its large Québécois population, was a hotbed of political activity for French Canadian expatriates. Riel's death fired up patriotic feelings in that centre of Franco-Americanism, and an organization called La Ligue des patriotes was formed there with the mission of defending the rights and interests of French Canadians in the United States. Lavallée composed an ultra-patriotic song for them called "Restons français" (Let's remain French)—a high-complexioned, stirring call to arms full of martial rhythms and extravagant lyrics ("The sky is black, the storm grows near, and discord lights up its torch"). All his life, Lavallée was ready to aid in nationalistic French sentiment—he never expressed himself politically in words, but he did so in art, several times.

Lavallée achieved some of his greatest artistic and organizational successes while living in Boston. He resumed consistent activity as a composer, working on an oratorio in 1886 and, calling on his minstrel and regimental roots, publishing three popular band marches in the same year. One publisher predicted that such marches might make him a fortune were he inclined to move his compositional efforts in that direction. But he was not so inclined. "I would rather be remembered for a few artistic compositions than to grow rich in other lines of musical effort," he was said to have replied (the piano manufacturer Henry F. Miller later recounted the story to a New York music journal). And there's no question he was serious about that sentiment. He chose his compositions selectively, including a commission to write a piece commemorating the unveiling of a statue of a former Boston mayor, part of a major public festival. He performed regularly and to generally good reviews.

Meanwhile, his position of leadership within the Music Teachers National Association became one of the pillars of his musical life. After his groundbreaking piano recital in 1884 and his presentation of the first all-American orchestral concert in 1885, he had been selected as chair of the program committee for the MTNA annual meeting for 1886, to be held in his hometown of Boston. Lavallée had suggested that only American works be performed during all the convention's concerts, still a radical idea for the time. He was turned down—it was a bridge too far for his more conservative colleagues, but it is indicative of Lavallée's thinking on the subject. He was a pioneer, a risk-taker, a true believer. He began to plan the 1886 annual meeting in earnest.

The Boston meeting was doubly significant to Lavallée because one of the most important projects of the Music Teachers National Association was the creation of the American College of Musicians, a body that would establish criteria for a professional teaching cadre in the United States, conferring certificates to prospective teachers, and act as a sort of professional regulatory association—very similar to the idea for a national conservatory that Lavallée had proposed for Quebec. And, as in Quebec, there was much opposition to this scheme among many of America's existing music teachers. Any proposal calling for the increased professionalization of music education struck fear in the hearts of a well-established, conservative group of music teachers and conservatory owners who were delighted with, and profited by, the state of instruction just as it was. They saw increasing demands for professional qualifications as a direct threat to their status and livelihood. Chief among these was the prestigious New England Conservatory of Music, which became a staunch opponent of the MTNA. Much of this opposition was centred in Boston, so the 1886 MTNA meeting in that city was expected to be a battleground.

Lavallée worked to ensure that the July 1886 convention would be one of the most extravagant, best attended, and most successful in the MTNA's history. To prepare Boston's musical establishment and the public for the American music they would hear that summer, Lavallée organized a series of public concerts in the spring of 1886, performed mainly by himself. Included in these concerts was a major composition of Lavallée's that has since been lost but which gathered a great deal of positive reaction in his lifetime: his Suite for Piano and Cello, op. 40. It is one of the great might-have-beens in Lavallée's body of work, a serious composition that might have achieved classic status.

Despite the opposition to the American College of Musicians, the 1886 Boston meeting was a great success, on the basis of which Lavallée was elected president of the MTNA for the next year. S.N. Penfield, the outgoing president, had nominated him in these terms:

You may refer to last year, when American compositions were given in a very worthy manner at the Academy of Music in New York. . . . But what led up to that? One modest piano recital of the year before by a gentleman who staked his reputation upon it. . . . I have the honour to present, as your candidate for the presidency in the ensuing year, the gentleman who gave that recital, Mr. Calixa Lavallée.

Lavallée's ascendancy within the Music Teachers National Association was not without its controversies. The first was a predictable jab at his nationality and religion. How could a Canadian, and a Catholic at that, be permitted to be a representative for American music? This was a question that surfaced immediately in the Boston press and was just as quickly dispatched by Lavallée's supporters. The more serious criticism revolved around the fact that Lavallée and many other members of the MTNA had demonstration contracts with piano manufacturers, which allowed their opponents to claim that they were acting solely in the interests of those manufacturers. Lavallée took steps within the association during his presidency to ensure that these conflicts of interest were kept to a minimum, if not entirely eliminated.

The personal criticism surrounding Lavallée came to a head during one of the greatest triumphs of his association with the MTNA. He had been selected to represent the group for the first time at a meeting of its British equivalent, the National Society of Professional Musicians, in January of 1888 in London. It was quite an occasion. Lavallée was the guest of honour, performing for the group and giving the keynote address, which was a history of American music. He was featured in several British journals, and his keynote speech was published in full in the press. Not bad for a kid from Verchères, Quebec.

But on his return to the United States, he bore the brunt of much criticism, some of it quite vicious. George Wilson of the *Boston Traveller* wrote, "We are very sorry Mr. Lavallée went to London; with the kindest of feelings for him personally, he must not be taken as a representative American musician, and we trust neither his music nor his address will get into type in the queen's country." That is, he was not a native-born American, and his views must not be taken as representative of American musicians. Lavallée must have felt in a double bind. In Canada, he had great personal credibility, but no one took his idea of a national conservatory seriously. In the United States, the conservatory idea was given real consideration, but he himself was deemed illegitimate. He couldn't win either way. The criticism over his visit to London resurfaced during the MTNA annual meeting in the summer of 1888, held this time in Chicago.

During this period of intense compositional and organizing activity, Lavallée seemed frail to many of his contemporaries. His health had actually begun to deteriorate around 1885, when he was forty-three. He had had throat problems for many years, and the overwhelming workload he imposed upon himself was no doubt a contributing factor to his physical weakening. More than one Boston newspaper cautioned him to take a break and do less. He didn't heed their advice. As well as leading the charge on behalf of American composers and compositions, Lavallée was also continuing a full teaching load, his main source of income, as well as writing a fair bit of music. In addition, he was made musical director of Boston's prestigious Cathedral of the Holy Cross in 1889—"perhaps the most important musical church appointment in New England," according to the *Musical Courier*— and he continued to contribute articles and reviews to several musical publications.

In the midst of all these efforts, which made Lavallée one of the best-known musicians in Boston (and prominent further afield), he visited Montreal in May of 1888. A group of travelling musicians had come to Boston from Quebec in the spring of 1887, and arrangements had been made then for Lavallée to return to Montreal for a concert visit. It was the first time he had set foot in Canada since the fall of 1880; it would be the last. One would like to believe that the concerts he performed in Montreal had special significance for Lavallée, and maybe they did. Lavallée's arrival in Montreal coincided with a speaking tour by Gabriel Dumont, the Métis leader who had been an ally of Louis Riel—a reminder of how much more complex and knotty the political situation in Canada and Quebec had become since Lavallée and Routhier had written their national hymn. The tensions within the country, exacerbated by the North-West Rebellion and especially by Riel's execution, had intensified the many cultural and racial hatreds that had been stirring under the surface for a generation. Now they were a malodorous presence, overwhelming the political scene. Dumont and Lavallée, two stars in the French Canadian firmament for different reasons, were given a joint reception in Montreal during their May appearance. Lavallée's concerts were presented on the following two days and received prominent notice in the press. But nothing more—Lavallée was probably in Montreal for a weekend. By Tuesday, he was back in Boston.

Sadly, by then Lavallée had just over two years left. At the 1887 convention of the MTNA in Indianapolis, his health had prevented him from taking the chair, even though he was president of the association at the time. After opening the assembly, he had spent the rest of the conference in his hotel room. Photographs from the late 1880s show a thin and tired Lavallée, but still with the piercing eyes which look out from every portrait, lithograph, photograph, and engraving of him from the time he was nineteen up to the age of forty-eight. But by 1889, those eyes are sunk into an exhausted face, puffy and gaunt. Lavallée pulled himself together enough to attend the 1890 MTNA conference in Detroit, and was selected once again to be head of the program committee for the 1892 convention in Cleveland. He never had a chance to finish the assignment. In October of 1890, he was seeing his doctor on a regular basis, and the throat disease—maybe tuberculosis, maybe cancer—was well on the way to ending his active and fruitful life. He died on the night of January 21, 1891, just a few weeks after his forty-eighth birthday. At his bedside, along with his wife and his brother Charles, was Léon Derome, the Montreal butcher who had first brought Lavallée to that city as a boy of twelve, virtually adopted him, and helped him begin his career. It was he who had raised the funds to send Lavallée to Paris and who had likely under-written the performances of *Jeanne d'Arc* in the 1870s, and he had clearly remained a lifelong friend and supporter. Derome was there when Lavallée was laid to rest on January 24 in the cemetery of the Cathedral of the Holy Cross, Boston's most prestigious church, where he had been choir director. A wreath at the funeral was inscribed, "The Friend of American Composers of Music."

In its obituary for the composer, *L'indépendant* of Fall River, a community so close to Lavallée's heart, remembered him in his role as leader of the French Canadian community: "His individu-ality made a profound mark in our memories: Congenial com-panion, charming conversationalist, open heart, candid nature, an industrious artist with the highest ideals." The *Musical Courier*, long a Lavallée champion, wrote that many would remember his "characteristic salutation, hearty, unaffected, with just a tinge of the Gallic in his pronunciation, and no little of the Gallic impetu-osity in his temperament." The French music journal *Le ménestrel* wrote, "Music in the United States is mourning the loss of one of its strongest supporters." Through these tributes, a portrait emerges of a man who was determined, gregarious, restless, a risk-taker—the same qualities we have seen throughout his life.

But perhaps the fullest appreciation of Lavallée—of the American Lavallée, that is—came during a meeting of the very association to which he had given so much energy. In the summer of 1892, at the annual convention of the Music Teachers National Association in Cleveland, the then president, J.B. Hahn, summed up Lavallée's achievements in this way:

> It was in this city—yes, in this very hall, eight years ago, that Calixa Lavallée sounded the keynote of a movement whose reverberations found a re-echoing and a responsive sentiment throughout the length and breadth of the land. Many here today will readily remember the occasion—a modest, unpretentious pianoforte recital, with the distinguishing characteristic that it was the first complete program of American compositions ever presented. The train of results which have sprung there from has been far-reaching beyond the wildest expectations.
>
> Lavallée's great strength with his brother musicians was the entire absence of jealousy; he worked for all, without favoritism, always persevering, and with great patriotism, sacrificing oftentimes his own interests for the sake of advancing the cause so dear to him. . . .
>
> For his patriotism, his courage, his judicious selection which led to victory and the leadership he then assumed, all honor to our late associate and ex-president, Calixa Lavallée, the Lafayette of our American musicians.

J.B. Hahn spoke eloquently of Lavallée from his limited perspective as an American musician. He had no way of knowing that his words about Lavallée working "with great patriotism . . . for the sake of advancing the cause so dear to him" also summed up perfectly Lavallée's relationship with his native country, in light of his heroic efforts to create the foundation for a professional musical culture in Quebec. It is one of the ironies of Lavallée's life that it was in a country not his own that he was able to most fully realize the plans and hopes he had formulated for his native province twenty years earlier—an ideal of using music as a potent force in national life, as a means of unifying a country and identifying its spiritual centre. This was the great purpose to which he had directed five years of effort in Quebec and ten years in Boston. In the end, in his adopted country, those efforts finally bore fruit.

And then the other irony: a two-minute song he wrote in a few weeks in 1880 to celebrate the French fact in Canada, afterwards largely forgotten by everyone including the composer himself, emerged from the shadows to become a national song—not of the nation it had been written for, but of the larger country which eventually claimed Lavallée as one of its own. That song, through its inner beauty and power, has inspired millions over a century—and become the anthem of a modern, progressive, forward-thinking country. A tune raised to the level of a symbol that soars in sound through a nation's imagination.

ELEVEN

IT MAY BE ONE of the great ironies of Canadian history that our national anthem was created and bequeathed to us by the spirit of Quebec nationalism—specifically by Quebec's Saint-Jean-Baptiste Society. No other organization in Quebec history has been more overtly nationalistic, nor has any so powerfully rallied the forces of Québécois independence and pride. It is the organization that made its founding date, the twenty-fourth of June, into Quebec's national holiday. Its symbol—the fleur-de-lys—made its way onto the Quebec flag. That it would be this institution—so fanatically faithful to the idea of the nation of Quebec and so opposed to the idea of the nation of Canada—that created Canada's national anthem must go down as one of the greater cosmic political jokes in Western history. Surely if it were not for an accident of language—that the name French Canadians give to their homeland, *Canada*, is the same one all Canadians give to theirs—this would not have been possible. "O Canada" is one of those tricks of the tongue—words that can mean two quite different things in two quite different contexts.

But, ultimately, the fact that a French Canadian national hymn could become the anthem for the entire country comes down to one thing, and one thing alone—the beauty of the music that Calixa Lavallée wrote for the song. Many different words have been sung to that melody, especially in English. The tune never changes, nor does it need to. No matter the lyrics, the anthem still casts the same fascination.

Nonetheless, it was a long haul for "O Canada" to reach the place it now occupies in the national imagination. It is a fascinating story, full of the twists and turns and accommodations and compromises that the country itself performed in the hundred years that passed between the writing of the song and its proclamation as our official national anthem. If "O Canada" began its life in French Canada, it ended up belonging to the nation as a whole.

And even in French Canada, "O Canada" wasn't immediately taken up as an anthem. Despite myth-making stories made up in later decades, the song was not heard a great deal within French Canada until the beginning of the twentieth century, twenty years after its composition, and even then it was not necessarily given pride of place. Neither Lavallée's obituary in 1891 nor Routhier's in 1920 mentions the piece at all. It did not appear in either the 1890 or the 1895 edition of the *Nouvelle lyre canadienne*, a collection of national songs. It was only in the twentieth century, around the time that English Canada was discovering the song, that French Canada began to perform it with regularity.

The claiming of "O Canada" in English Canada took a long time as well. For one thing, English Canada thought it already had its own national song in the late nineteenth century. "The Maple Leaf Forever" had been written by Alexander Muir in 1867 to commemorate Confederation. The song had just enough of a patriotic lilt to its unusual melody to solidify its emotional ties with several generations of English Canadians, well into the first decades of the twentieth century. However, its lyrics, like those of Lorne's "Dominion Hymn," are unintentionally demonstrative of exactly the kind of cultural rifts that have made the unity of Canada so fragile. What other putative national anthem celebrates the military humiliation of one part of the country by another?

> In days of yore, from Britain's shore,
> Wolfe the dauntless hero came,
> And planted firm Britannia's flag
> On Canada's fair domain.
> Here may it wave, our boast and pride . . .

"The Maple Leaf Forever" speaks louder than it intends to. It speaks of the insensitive, anglocentric Canada of the late decades of the nineteenth century—a country sure of itself, looking back to a British heritage to give itself strength and purpose, completely unaware and uninterested in the French reality of the country. The song is a portrait of exactly the kind of myopia that has always threatened the unity of the Dominion.

But it's a powerful song nonetheless, lyrics be damned. If "The Maple Leaf Forever" was going to be dethroned, it wasn't going to be by arguments about cultural sensitivity. The battle was going to be fought in the musical hearts and minds of Canadians.

And of course there was another rival to "O Canada," a more potent one, which lasted well into the 1970s—"God Save the Queen" (or "King," depending on the era). Unlike the contest between "The Maple Leaf Forever" and "O Canada," which was eventually a question of which had the better tune and more stirring lyrics, the battle between "God Save the Queen" and "O Canada" has always been ideological. It is a contest between two different ways of seeing and understanding the country. "God Save the Queen" allows us to hear in its very words and notes our debt to Great Britain, our connection to and love of the "mother country." It's a powerful evocation of an emotional tie that is particularly strong.

"O Canada," on the other hand, represents our independence as a nation as a source of pride; it is focused on the future more than the past, on our collective accomplishments rather than on the heritage we were bequeathed. It depicts a sense of freedom and autonomy that first developed in French Canada and has since spread to the rest of the country. In a very real way, "O Canada" was waiting for those of us in the rest of Canada to feel its need, to feel the spirit of self-determination that it celebrates not just in its lyrics but, mysteriously, in the music itself, in that odd combination of hymn and march, reverence and determination, pride and power that is its hallmark. Like so many other aspects of Canadian life, something that emerged first in French Canada—a sense of connection to this land, a sense of destiny—has ended up extending itself to the rest of the country. Whether acknowledged or not, French Canada has been the incubator of much authentic Canadian experience. "O Canada" is one example.

...

The long journey that "O Canada" took to become English Canada's national anthem began in 1901. That was the first time the piece was heard outside of Quebec, at ceremonies welcoming the Duke and Duchess of Cornwall and York (later George V and Queen Mary) to Toronto. It had been played earlier in the royal visit as well, in Quebec City, by a band led by Joseph Vézina (a Lavallée pupil). The song's introduction to English Canada, along with its re-emergence into French Canada after a twenty-one-year hiatus, seems to date from this royal tour. The piece was published in Quebec soon after the tour, and it started to get better known throughout that province as well.

The next milestone for "O Canada" in English came five years later, in 1906, when the Toronto Mendelssohn Choir, which had taken part in the 1901 royal tour, added Lavallée's composition to their ongoing repertoire and sang it several times in Toronto as well as on tour in Pittsburgh. The Toronto *Globe*, in February 1907, called the piece "a popular hit" which "stirred the patriotic feelings of the audience, and was tumultuously encored." "O Canada" was on its way in English Canada.

With one small hitch. English Canadian audiences weren't going to listen to the song with its original French lyrics, which they couldn't understand. And there were no original English lyrics to "O Canada," as we know. So, as the song became better and better known in English-speaking Canada, the need for English words became a pressing problem.

The audiences of the Mendelssohn Choir in 1906 heard the first of dozens, if not hundreds or even thousands, of versions of "O Canada" that have been paraded across the English Canadian stage since the first decade of the twentieth century. We're still arguing about the words—the last change in the lyrics was approved by Parliament in 2018. The saga of the English lyrics to "O Canada" is at once amusing and extremely revealing. We can't change the melody of the song, and the French words are untouchable, beyond us. So discussing, arguing about, contemplating, reworking the English words to "O Canada" has been one of the sideshows to a much larger battle within the country over the past century or so: defining the nation itself. As crazy as it may seem, choosing the words to Lavallée's little song has opened a window—a revealing one—into exactly who we are as a country, and who we want to be.

The original English words to "O Canada," the ones the Mendelssohn Choir sang in 1906, were written by a Toronto physician named Thomas Bedford Richardson. Richardson's version, called "Our Fathers' Land of Old," was essentially a translation of Routhier's original French lyrics, with "our fathers' land of old" as a rendering of "terre de nos aïeux." But a direct translation of the ultramontane Catholic sentiments that underlie the original words to "O Canada" caused something of a sensation, and not a positive one, in the British and Protestant stronghold of Ontario. No one in English Canada was going to sing this:

O Canada! Our fathers' land of old,
Thy brow is crown'd with leaves of red and gold.
Beneath the shade of the Holy Cross
Thy children own their birth,
No stains thy glorious annals gloss
Since valour shield thy hearth.
Almighty God! On thee we call,
Defend our rights, forfend this nation's thrall,
Defend our rights, forfend this nation's thrall.

Forget the unlikelihood of our Olympic athletes standing on some gold-medal podium somewhere, singing lustily, "forfend this nation's thrall." The Richardson lyrics failed because they did their job all too well—they were a too-faithful rendition of the aggressively Catholic Routhier original. Something else was needed, and needed quickly, if the music of "O Canada," which everyone loved, was to remain a permanent part of the English Canadian landscape. And the new words could not simply be a better translation. A brand-new set of lyrics was needed. But what could they possibly be? And who should write them?

Collier's magazine, one of the most popular and influential newsweeklies of its time, had an idea. To launch its Canadian edition in the fall of 1908, it sponsored a contest for new English lyrics for "O Canada." It received over 350 entries, judged them all, and in August of 1909 announced that its winner was one Mrs. Mercy E. Powell McCulloch of British Columbia. Her winning entry wasn't terrible, but neither was it especially inspiring:

O Canada! In praise of thee we sing;
From echoing hills our anthems proudly ring.
With fertile plains and mountains grand
With lakes and rivers clear,
Eternal beauty, thou dost stand
Throughout the changing year.
Lord God of Hosts! We now implore
Bless our dear land this day and evermore,
Bless our dear land this day and evermore.

Like so many of the *Collier's* entries, Mrs. McCulloch's words stress the natural beauty of Canada—one of the few unifying themes that emerge again and again among the candidates. And the competition, with its hundreds of entries, brought every possible set of lyrics for "O Canada" out of the woodwork. Toronto critic Augustus Brindle tried his hand at them, as did the poet Wilfred Campbell. Ewing Buchan, a bank manager in Vancouver, wrote a set that became extremely popular in British Columbia:

O Canada, our heritage, our love
Thy worth we praise all other lands above.
From sea to sea throughout their length
From Pole to borderland,

At Britain's side, whate'er betide
Unflinchingly we'll stand.
With heart we sing, "God Save the King"
Guide thou the Empire wide, do we implore,
And prosper Canada from shore to shore.

All of these examples demonstrate how difficult it is to come up with just the right language and tone for a song destined to be a symbolic talisman for a large group of disparate people. What unifies us as a country? And, more to the point, what unified us in 1908, just forty years after Confederation? As we can see, the major themes that emerged at the time were the beauty of the landscape and the legacy of British culture in the country. English Canada was still shedding its colonial past in the first decade of the twentieth century, and the weakness of the early English lyrics to "O Canada" was a reflection of our still-developing, still-nascent culture. The French lyrics, on the other hand, express much more powerful sentiments. They speak of history, continuity, glory, faith, common values, and rights. "O Canada" in French has plenty to talk about other than the natural beauty of the country. It has a homeland to reflect, a country of the heart, and memory and imagination and pride. In 1908, no such country yet existed for English Canadians.

So when one writer finally did manage to create English lyrics that resonated with the public, the achievement was thus all the more remarkable. That writer was Robert Stanley Weir, a judge from Montreal who was also something of a poet. In 1908, just before the *Collier's* contest, Weir retired to his summer home to write a set of English lyrics for "O Canada" for the three-hundredth-anniversary celebration of Quebec City. And with some changes and emendations—some made by the poet himself—the result was the anthem we sing today when we sing it in English. It was Weir who penned "O Canada! Our home and native land!"; Weir who commanded us to see the country "with glowing hearts" and as "the True North strong and free." For possibly the first time among the hundreds of English-language versions of the song, something approaching true poetry broke out.

But the real success of Weir's version was its faithfulness to the spirit of Lavallée and Routhier's original, without being a direct translation of its lyrics. Surely the fact that Weir lived in Montreal, albeit English Montreal, made him more sensitive to the original French Canadian significance of the anthem. Still, it took him a few tries to get there. The original poem Weir wrote for "O Canada" was in three stanzas, although hardly anyone ever reads or sings the second or the third. The first stanza and the refrain, which eventually became the version we sing today, read as follows:

O Canada! Our home and native land!
True patriot love thou dost in us command.
We see thee rising fair, dear land,
The True North strong and free;
And stand on guard, O Canada,
We stand on guard for thee.

O Canada! O Canada!
O Canada! We stand on guard for thee.
O Canada! We stand on guard for thee.

An attentive reader may notice a few surprising things about this early version. The first is that the line "true patriot love in all thy sons command," which has been the source of so much controversy over the years, isn't there in the original. Although "true patriot love thou dost in us command" may be a bit fusty and

Victorian, it's at least gender-neutral. Weir himself changed the lyrics to the more familiar "in all thy sons command" in 1913, just before the First World War. Exactly why, no one is sure. People have been arguing about the change more or less from the time he made it more than a hundred years ago.

As well, the lovely phrase "with glowing hearts we see thee rise," maybe the finest of the song, is also missing. Weir edited it in himself in one of his three revisions, each of which made significant improvements on his original. "We see thee rising fair, dear land" is just too wimpy. One wonders whether we'd still be singing his words if he hadn't made that change. And finally, it's hard not to notice that there's a lot of standing on guard in the first Weir version. It's as though his inspiration failed him after that fine phrase "the True North strong and free." From that point to the end of the refrain, it's just "O Canada!" (five of them) and some version of standing on guard for thee (four). Kind of boring.

Weir himself eliminated some of those repetitions in his revisions; subsequent editors took care of the others. In fact, as we'll see, those closing words of the anthem have undergone more tinkering than any others in the song. Weir made the first change himself, an excellent one, adding the words "glorious and free" to replace one "O Canada," so that the first line of the refrain read "O Canada! Glorious and free!" In 1968, that first "O Canada" disappeared as well, and the line became "God keep our land glorious and free!" Finally, after "the True North strong and free," the words became "from far and wide, O Canada," instead of "and stand on guard, O Canada." (Although when I first sang the anthem, in the 1950s, I'm pretty sure the last lines were, "O Canada! Glorious and free! / We stand on guard, we stand on guard for thee. / O Canada, we stand on guard for thee." You can determine the age of a Canadian within a few months by asking them what version of the anthem they sang in public school!)

The original English lyrics have been manhandled quite a bit over the years, but even with all the changes, we can see why the Weir version stuck when so many others fell by the wayside. Weir was a Quebecer and thus understood the spirit of the original "O Canada," and he was able to reflect it back in his version. Not literally, word by word, but with emotional acuity. And Weir, almost alone of all the potential English lyricists, understood the sound of Lavallée's music, the meaning behind it.

Weir's cleverness in combining a respect for the spirit of the original with an understanding of the new audience he was writing for is evident from the first line of his version. "O Canada! Our home and native land!" is not a direct translation of the central invocation of the Routhier original, "Ô Canada! Terre de nos aïeux," but it's a gesture towards it, a rooting of patriotic feeling in the land and in the emotions surrounding the idea of home. It centres the anthem in feeling, in sentimentality, without invoking the idea of ancestors that was so key to the French conception of "O Canada." Weir understood that such an idea was less meaningful in English Canada, where the ancestors of many, if not most, of its inhabitants come from someplace else.

Weir's insightful treatment of the original continues in the middle section, with its insistent rhythm that accompanies the original French words "Car ton bras sait porter l'épée, / Il sait porter la croix." It's a critical part of the song; it plays a key role in the music's success. This is where Lavallée moves from hymn to march, from the divine to the mundane, from the next world to this one. Weir has caught that spirit in his revised words, "With glowing hearts we see thee rise, / The True North strong and free!" Like a mist coming off a northern lake, Canada appears before us, inspiring a nation and calling forth a determined response. But there is a hint of militarism here as well, drawn right from the music of this section. Weir hears the martial charge in Lavallée's score and puts us on notice: "And stand on guard, O Canada, / We stand on guard for thee." (The revision from "and stand on guard, O Canada" to "from far and wide, O Canada" weakens the lyrics precisely because it loosens that martial spirit.) Again, without directly translating the French words, Weir hints at the same sentiment they express—a need for Canadians to defend their country's values, by force of arms if necessary—but now the desire to defend the country has a secular motivation, not a religious one. Finally, to top off this middle section, Weir actually does Routhier one better—he mimics Lavallée's music, matching "we see thee rise" with the rising and falling figure that Lavallée wrote into the score.

Weir also shows his attunement to the spirit of the French version by preserving Routhier's original conceit, the direct address to Canada. It's something we hardly notice in "O Canada," but we are singing to the country itself. This is especially clear in the French original; Routhier is always addressing Canada in the second person, as a friendly and almost maternal spirit. It's a love letter to a nation:

O Canada! Home of *our* ancestors,
Your brow is garlanded with glorious flowers!
Because *your* arm knows how to wield the sword,
It knows how to carry the cross!
Your history is an epic
Of brilliant deeds.
And *your* valour, steeped in faith,
Will protect *our* homes and *our* rights.

The original, French "O Canada" is like an invocation to an ancient god or goddess—*you are wonderful, and you are our protector.* It creates an intimate and powerful relationship between the person singing the song and the country to which it is sung.

Weir seems conscious of this intimacy in his version of the anthem, though he cannot in English be as familiar with the country as Routhier could be in French. English Canada, the embryo of the Canada we have today, was essentially unformed in 1908—open, waiting, masked by the future. Those who inhabited it did not have enough history with the nation to address it in the same personal terms as French Canada could. In Weir's lyrics, we give to Canada, we pledge our allegiance to it, but we don't make demands of it. It makes demands of us—"true patriot love thou dost in us command"—and we deliver: "we stand on guard for thee." In French, we lionize and celebrate Canada, and we call on it to protect us. In English, we acknowledge the country as something slightly separate and distant from us, but we vow to protect it. The relationship is reversed.

It's a subtle shift, but significant psychologically—it speaks to the deep-seated alienation that has always been part of the English Canadian personality. In Weir's version of English Canada, the country owes us nothing—it is beautiful and glorious but also silent, aloof. We respect and honour it, are moved by it (with glowing hearts), and pledge to protect it, but we are separate from it. Routhier, on the other hand, smothers his Canada with honour and glory and calls on it for protection; the connection French Canadians have with their country is all-sustaining. Thus, Canada is entangled in an emotional relationship in the French version of the anthem, but it stands solitary and alone in the English version. It is an important difference. And it's the reason the other change to the original Weir lyrics, the addition in 1968 of "God keep our land glorious and free!," rings so false. In the original English text, in contrast with the French version, God has nothing to do with our relationship to our country. Canada is "glorious and free" by its own nature, alone and proud in the universe. It is we Canadians who have the responsibility to keep it that way, not God. We can depend on nothing but our own instincts, our own pride, our own vigilance. We are alone, and that solitude is thrilling.

. . .

Weir's lyrics first appeared in 1908, were amended by him three times—in 1909, 1913, and 1916—and soon became the generally accepted English version of the anthem. Year by year, "O Canada" became more prominent in English Canada as a national song, increasingly played on ceremonial occasions, and "The Maple Leaf Forever" started to recede in popularity. At the beginning of the First World War, the two pieces were vying for supremacy on something of an equal footing. However, by 1924, the Association of Canadian Clubs had declared "O Canada" to be their official song. In 1927, it was officially published by the Government of Canada to commemorate the sixtieth anniversary of Confederation. The Peace Tower Carillon on Parliament Hill, newly installed that same year, pealed out "O Canada" as its first-ever music. "O Canada" had begun to establish itself as English Canada's unofficial anthem, with "God Save the King" a constant, at times confusing, presence in the background.

It's no surprise that this momentum for "O Canada" began in the 1920s and 1930s. Those were the decades when so much Canadian nationalism first took hold, as the country loosened its ties to its British roots. This was the period that produced the first great wave of Canadian historical scholarship, in the work of

Harold Innis and Donald Creighton, as well as the Statute of Westminster (1931), Canada's true declaration of independence from Great Britain. It was an era of increasing Canadian pride and confidence, following our military experiences in the First World War. Those years even gave us our first major cultural expression of ourselves: a national public broadcaster, the CBC.

The rise of "O Canada" paralleled these developments in English Canada—in fact, the song is their symbol. In French Canada, the anthem stands as an expression of nationalist feeling that roots itself in a history stretching back to the seventeenth century. It is a statement of past glories and future wariness, a key element in *la survivance*. It is about keeping alive something precious from times past. In English Canada, by contrast, "O Canada" has always represented the future. It was the symbol and the banner under which the country embraced not its past but its present, and the extension of that present into the future. It depicts a country which finds its identity in what is yet to come. Thus "O Canada" in English is completely Canadian, independent of all colonial ties. In that respect, it is like the French version—in effect, it was this evocation of a country with its own free will that allowed the two anthems to eventually merge into one.

But in English Canada, that view of Canada as a free and independent nation was challenged, well into the twentieth century, by a de facto imperialist vision of the country which stressed its connections to Great Britain—especially its cultural connections, which persisted long after the primary economic ties to the metropolitan centre had atrophied. For those who loved, cherished, and honoured that imperial heritage, and for whom "God Save the Queen" was the ultimate musical symbol, "O Canada" represented something almost indecent—a harbinger of the abandonment of history, of security, of the natural order of things. For these

Canadians, turning away from Britain was as unnatural as denying your own DNA. As well, they believed (not incorrectly) that the British connection had been and continued to be the key to Canada's independence. Britain protected Canada from the rest of the world, gave it meaning, and especially helped it repel the advances of its aggressive neighbour to the south. It might be a fine song, but "O Canada" did not express the historical ground of the country as these Canadians saw it, did not honour the essential unity that Canada enjoyed with Great Britain, the politico-biological connection to the mother country.

For this reason, "O Canada" was embattled in its journey to becoming the official national anthem of English Canada in a way that it had never been in French Canada. Routhier and Lavallée's "Ô Canada" stood at the end of a long process of cultural development in Quebec, and thus its acceptance as a national symbol was a fait accompli. In English, "O Canada" stood at the beginning of that process of development, and the direction it signalled was not entirely acceptable to all of its citizens. The battle around proclaiming it our official anthem came to symbolize an existential contest between two different conceptions of the country, and it thus embodies the modern history of Canada as few other controversies have.

TWELVE

I F "O CANADA" WAS ALREADY Canada's de facto national anthem by 1927, it remained an unofficial one for the better part of the twentieth century. The process to make it official was longer and more arduous than anyone could have imagined. The first proposal to attempt to do so was tabled in the Canadian Parliament in 1962 as a private member's bill by Pierre Sévigny, a minister in the government of John Diefenbaker. Eighteen years and five governments later, that proposal was finally approved. It took a dozen failed measures and bills before "O Canada" became the official national anthem in 1980, the centenary of its composition. And changes to the official version are still being regularly proposed, with some being implemented—the last being the bill passed in the Commons in 2016, but not ratified by the Senate until 2018, which returned gender neutrality to Robert Weir's famous second line by changing "in all thy sons command" to "in all of us command." The anthem, supposed symbol of our unity, has been surprisingly divisive over the decades.

Why such a long time and such a tortuous process? Because an anthem is more than just a simple song. As a national symbol, it is understood to stand for something greater than itself, for political forces and historical trends deep within the country's soul and past. An anthem is never just a collection of notes and words—it is one of the beating hearts of a country, watched over with great concern and care. Debates about the anthem are always about something else—about values that are considered central to the nation. We can see in the parliamentary battles over "O Canada" a revealing X-ray of our developing Canadian identity—a process that has of necessity produced a great deal of anxiety, anger, passion, and confusion as it seeks a form of unity.

And unity is what "O Canada" was supposed to be about. By the 1940s, everyone in the country knew the anthem, and most responded positively to it. Miraculously, it was acceptable to both linguistic communities. Having long been important in French Canada, it had become beloved on the English side as well. It had won the hearts and minds of citizens all across the country. It should have been an easy lay-up to get it official status.

It wasn't.

Blame Lester B. Pearson, if you like, for the original naïveté about getting "O Canada" official status. It was Pearson's government that really started the ball rolling to make "O Canada" the official national anthem in the early 1960s, that Liberal administration responsible for establishing so much of the modern foundation of the country, from the Canada Pension Plan to medicare to the flag. By 1963, the privation of the war years and the stuffiness of the fifties were waning, and a new generation of young people—the baby boomers—were coming of age. There was a new confidence astir in North America, accelerated in Canada by the impending centennial of Confederation and the burgeoning pride at hosting the Expo 67 World's Fair planned for Montreal. In Quebec, a century of stultifying ecclesiastical control of the province was being replaced by a forward-looking, vigorous flexing of political and cultural muscle that went by the name of the Quiet Revolution. The Royal Commission on Bilingualism and Biculturalism was just in the wings. Pearson and the Liberal party were working to create the foundations of a strong, modern country, and they felt they needed new symbols to represent it. That's where "O Canada" was supposed to fit in.

The desire to make "O Canada" the official anthem was linked right from the beginning with the more contentious proposal to create a new flag for Canada—or first flag, depending on which side of the debate you were on. The Red Ensign, with its incorporation of the British Union Jack, was Canada's unofficial flag, but Pearson felt it was time for Canada to have a national flag and symbol of its own. The government announced its intentions on both fronts—flag and anthem—in its Throne Speech in May of 1963. The two seemed to go hand in hand. As one MP, Henri Latulippe, said, "If we adopt a distinctive Canadian flag, we should also proclaim a distinctive national anthem, for we could not very well look at our distinctive national flag and, at the same time, sing the national anthem of another country."

Early debate on the anthem focused on the relative merits of "O Canada" and "God Save the Queen." The argument for "O Canada" was put simply but effectively by, among others, Red Kelly, former member of the Detroit Red Wings and Toronto Maple Leafs, who had recently been elected to Parliament. In his maiden speech, replying to the Speech from the Throne, Kelly noted that when he had travelled abroad with his team and heard "God Save the Queen" played before an international game, he hadn't felt much. However, in recent years, he said, "'O Canada' has been played the odd time. As I have stood before these people in a foreign country and they started to play and sing 'O Canada, our home and native land,' I have felt great pride and my chest stood out a little more. They were singing about our land, our home."

Debate on both the new Canadian flag and the adoption of "O Canada" as our national anthem became more heated in May of 1964, when the Pearson government formally introduced their twin nation-building motions: one to approve the flag, the other to approve the anthem. They had decided to begin with the debate over the new flag, probably assuming that since that motion was asking Canadians to approve something brand new, it would be the more difficult and contentious of the two. They had every right to assume that making "O Canada" official would be something of a no-brainer, since Canadians had already been using it in a semi-official capacity for forty years.

They couldn't have been more mistaken. Oh yes, the flag debate was contentious, one of the most divisive and bitter controversies ever to play out in the halls of Parliament. The debate in the House of Commons alone went on for a remarkable six months—over three hundred speeches were passionately delivered, pro and con, on the topic between June and December of 1964. Insults were hurled, passions inflamed; our historic British past stood against an independent Canadian future. Half a year of trials and controversy and heat engulfed the nation. But, finally, Pearson had his way (he had to invoke closure to do so) and a new flag was raised in February of 1965, with a different design in the end than the one that had bitterly divided Parliament. It had taken the better part of a year, but it was done.

Now it was time to do the simpler thing—make "O Canada" the official national anthem. But that didn't take a year. Amazingly, it took almost two decades. This proves exactly how powerfully emotional music is, and how much more tenacious aural symbols are than visual ones. It was one thing to see the Union Jack or the

Red Ensign taken down and the Maple Leaf flag fly in its place—difficult, but not emotionally impossible. On the other hand, not to hear the familiar and enormously loved hymnal strains of "God Save the Queen" flowing before every hockey game or session of Parliament or any other formal occasion was, for many Canadians, too much to bear. They could lose the flag, but not so easily the song, even if it were to be replaced by something almost as familiar. It wasn't about familiarity—it was about emotion. And tradition.

Pearson's government had reluctantly accepted this fact after the turmoil of the flag debate. Another controversy over the anthem would threaten the very unity these new symbols were intended to create. So, rather than try tempers again in the House and in the country, the "O Canada" motion was referred to a special joint committee of the House and Senate to iron out any difficulties and report back. It never did. The motion just died on the order paper. Too controversial. So Canada got an official flag in 1965—but not an official anthem.

So Pearson tried again. If we couldn't have an official national anthem in time to sing along with the raising of our new flag, we could surely get one in time for Centennial year, the one hundredth anniversary of Confederation, in 1967. That gave Parliament almost two years to get the measure approved. It wasn't enough time. Even in 1967, in the midst of the swinging sixties, with Expo at full tilt and a sense of Canadian pride in the air, there was far from unanimous support in the country for "O Canada" as the official national anthem. In July, there was a near riot among the directors of the Canadian National Exhibition at their annual luncheon. When the chair called for the singing of the national anthem, half the assembly launched into "God Save the Queen," the other half into "O Canada." It took some time to calm down the proceedings. For many Canadians, replacing "God Save the Queen" was almost traitorous.

It wasn't until the summer of 1968, almost twelve months after Canada Day of Centennial year had come and gone, that legislative progress was actually made on "O Canada." It had been four years since the first motion to make "O Canada" the official anthem had been tabled in the House. The new flag had been flying for more than three years. Lester Pearson had retired from politics. And still no anthem.

In 1968, a new committee had been struck to figure out how to make "O Canada" official. And they actually got somewhere, although their deliberations sometimes verged on the comic. The main sticking point in the debate was the song's English lyrics (Parliament had actually approved the tune and the French lyrics back in 1967). As it turned out, close to a thousand Canadians had suggestions as to what those English lyrics should be. The committee members listened for weeks on end to different versions of the anthem. They hired a guitarist to play the tune for the various options. People came and sang for the MPs behind closed doors. It went on for months.

Finally, a breakthrough. For the first time, there was all-party agreement surrounding the issue. "O Canada" was to be the anthem, with Lavallée's music and Routhier's French words intact. As for the official English lyrics, they would be a reworking of those of Robert Stanley Weir—a relatively substantial reworking. It was this committee that added "from far and wide, O Canada" and "God keep our land " to Weir's original. The recommended text, then, became:

O Canada! Our home and native land!
True patriot love in all thy sons command.

With glowing hearts we see thee rise,
The True North strong and free!
From far and wide, O Canada,
We stand on guard for thee.
God keep our land glorious and free!
O Canada, we stand on guard for thee.
O Canada, we stand on guard for thee.

The committee's decision had been unanimous, joining Liberals, Conservatives, and New Democrats. Finally, four years after the first motion to make "O Canada" the official anthem had been tabled, a reasonable proposal to get the deed done had been introduced.

It didn't happen. Something interceded in the debate that no one had anticipated: when the new lyrics to "O Canada" were made public with the proposed changes, the family of Robert Stanley Weir, the author of the original English lyrics, decided they didn't like the changes one bit. They added a new wrinkle to the debate by claiming copyright over the original text. The government, they said, lacked the legal right to change the words at all. The lyrics didn't belong to them. They belonged to the Weir family.

It took a year and a half for lawyers to sort through the legal entanglements of copyright law as it applied to "O Canada." As it turned out, the Weir family did not actually control the copyright to "O Canada"; it had passed years before to the Gordon V. Thompson publishing firm. After long and complex negotiations, Thompson assigned the copyright to the Crown for one dollar. The copyright issue was solved—but it was now October of 1970. Finally, it seemed, the Liberal government, now under Pierre Trudeau, could proceed with this long-overdue measure. But Act Two of the "O Canada" drama was about to start.

As it turned out, despite their numerical ascendancy, the Liberals couldn't get the "O Canada" bill through Parliament. Yes, they had a majority government, but the pro-"God Save the Queen" sentiment was still so powerful in the country that using that majority would have had stinging political consequences. Various Liberal secretaries of state in the 1970s introduced bills to make "O Canada" the official anthem, but each was stymied by the divided public sentiment. Gérard Pelletier tried in 1972. The bill never got to second reading. Hugh Faulkner tried in 1974. No dice. John Roberts made an attempt in 1976. He tried again in 1977. In each instance, even though the Liberals could have bulled the bill through Parliament, they were afraid of the political consequences. In 1977, fourteen years after the Pearson government had first proposed it as the official national anthem, "O Canada" was still unofficial. At that point, the Liberals basically gave up trying.

Three years later, we were now in 1980, and ready for Act Three of the drama. Ten-odd years of Trudeau Liberalism and increasing Canadian national development had finally tempered the pro-monarchist forces in the country, and the "God Save the Queen" proponents were a little less vocal and intransigent. Meanwhile, it had been noted in the House in the early months of 1980 that "O Canada" was to have its centenary later that year, and Canada Post was preparing to introduce stamps featuring Lavallée, Routhier, and Weir. The idea of celebrating "O Canada" was in the air. But the government was still wary of trying to proceed to make it the official national anthem; they had tried so many times in the past without success, and they were in no hurry to raise another anthem-related hullabaloo. Even as the times had changed, they weren't confident of being able to overcome the dug-in resistance to the song that had been around since at least 1968.

Then fate intervened. On May 20, 1980, the people of Quebec, finally attaining a political maturity they had been anticipating since the Quiet Revolution of the 1960s, held the first referendum on Quebec sovereignty—or as it was called at that time, sovereignty-association. It was a vote that could have potentially split up the country, and the most serious existential threat the nation had faced at least since the conscription crises of the two World Wars, maybe even since the execution of Louis Riel. For the first time since Confederation, the possibility of Canada breaking apart and re-forming along the lines of its original linguistic communities was a real possibility. The mood in the country was fearful, anxious. The fate of the nation seemed to hang in the balance.

The forces of sovereignty lost that night. Sixty per cent of Quebecers decided not to pursue the sovereignty-association option. But at forty per cent, the anti-Canada vote was considerable. When René Lévesque, the premier of Quebec and the force behind the referendum, pledged to his assembled supporters in his concession speech, "À la prochaine"—until next time—there seemed little doubt that there would indeed be a next time. Likely sooner rather than later.

As Lévesque brought his speech to a close that night, something extraordinary happened in the arena in which he addressed his crestfallen supporters. In his hoarse, three-pack-a-day voice, he rallied the crowd to sing a song with him—"Gens du pays," a tune by Quebec folksinger Gilles Vigneault which had become the unofficial anthem of a separate Quebec. "Gens du pays, c'est votre tour" (People of the country, it's your turn) rose in a swelling wave through the space, crystallizing a feeling, an emotion, a political movement. It was a spine-tingling moment in Canadian history. A song speaking for a nation.

That hoarse, off-key rendition of "Gens du pays" galvanized Lévesque's supporters that Tuesday night—and it seems to have galvanized the Parliament of Canada as well, because by Friday of that same week, "O Canada" was miraculously on its way to finally being adopted as the official national anthem of Canada. It had been stalled for one reason after another since 1964, and now, in just over a month, it would be a fait accompli. Can we thank René Lévesque? Maybe.

As soon as the House of Commons was gavelled into order on Wednesday afternoon, the next day, Roch La Salle, the Conservative member from Joliette, had one idea of how the country could respond to the referendum and events in Quebec. He introduced an emergency motion calling on the government to make "O Canada" the national anthem as soon as possible. Under normal circumstances, these private motions were routinely ignored by the House. But this one passed instantly and unanimously. It was a portent of things to come.

The next day, another Conservative MP, Ron Stewart (not to be confused with the famous Ottawa Rough Riders running back), followed up La Salle's motion and introduced a private member's bill to make "O Canada" the national anthem. Stewart had introduced exactly the same bill the week before, but it had been denied the unanimous consent it needed to proceed because it made no recommendations at all about the English lyrics, which had been tying the Commons up in knots since 1968. In fact, the consent had been denied by none other than Prime Minister Trudeau himself, who yelled out "What are the words?" across the floor to Stewart. But that was last week, and this week, in the emotionally charged post-referendum House, things were very different. The bill, with all its flaws, might well have passed.

It's hard to tell reading Hansard thirty-some years later, but it looks like the Liberal government was taken completely off guard by Stewart's reintroduction of his bill. Secretary of State Francis

Fox was not in the House when Stewart made his motion, so he raced to get there, with other Liberal members vamping for time while he made his way to the chamber. With the results of the referendum looming over them, the Liberals didn't want to be seen to be killing the bill this time—but neither did they want it to pass. Finally, Fox hustled into the chamber just in time to offer Stewart a deal. If Stewart would agree to withdraw his bill, the Liberals would introduce one of their own as soon as possible to make the anthem official. Stewart agreed—and the die was cast that would make "O Canada" the country's official anthem.

Fox was as good as his word. On June 18, just three weeks later, he tabled his "O Canada" bill. It hadn't taken officials in the Department of Secretary of State very long to ready the legislation. The bill they introduced was exactly the same one, word for word, that they had introduced in 1968. And in 1972, 1974, 1976, and 1977. Never before had it had enough support to pass unanimously. Now—thanks to René Lévesque, the referendum, and perhaps "Gens du pays"—it did.

And so, on June 27, 1980, just four days before Canada Day, a remarkable scene played out on Parliament Hill. A bill that had been debated for years, that had occasioned the fiercest opposition, passed second and third readings in both the House and the Senate and received royal assent—all in a single day. In the early afternoon, Francis Fox had stood in the House to begin debate on the bill. By six o'clock, it was law. In proposing the bill, Fox spoke of an anthem as "the manifestation of a need, as well as the will, to belong to a group that is larger than the family cell or particular groups. It is also the manifestation of personal beliefs in values that are held as fundamental." In "O Canada," he said, we could "enshrine one of the most unifying realities of our young collective history." Fox was followed, in a nice gesture of generosity, not by the leader of the opposition as might be expected, but by Ron Stewart, the MP whose private member's bill had gotten the whole ball rolling just a few weeks earlier. Ed Broadbent, speaking for the NDP, noted the significance of the fact that "O Canada" had been written by a Quebecer, although no one present for the debate seems to have really understood the Quebec nationalist history in which the anthem was steeped. No matter. The day was one for unity and hope.

When the bill finally passed, Walter Baker, Conservative MP for Nepean–Carleton, rose to say, "On a point of order, Mr. Speaker, I think it would be quite appropriate if at this time the House sang the national anthem." So, French and English, Liberals, Conservatives, NDPers, members from Quebec and British Columbia and Ontario and Alberta—all stood and sang the song they all knew, some in French, some in English (but few likely using the just-approved official lyrics), some haltingly, some lustily. They sang the tune Calixa Lavallée had written a hundred years earlier, the tune that had come to symbolize a nation. Maybe some in the visitors' gallery joined in; maybe even some in the press gallery.

Were there tears? Hansard is silent on the subject. It would be hard to believe that there were not. Canada seemed to be finally doing something to protect its unity, to protect itself, to make a statement to the world about who it was. Four days later, on Canada Day, "O Canada" was officially proclaimed the national anthem by Governor General Ed Schreyer. The battle was finally over.

...

Except, of course, it wasn't.

Those pesky English lyrics were still a problem. The spirit of unity that the Quebec referendum had splashed over the country still couldn't erase major objections to the now-approved English version of the anthem. Some people didn't like "our home and native land" in the first line, noting that for an increasing number of Canadians, Canada wasn't their native land.

But the real sticking point in the official lyrics was the change that Robert Stanley Weir had made to his own original in 1913, changing "thou dost in us command" to "in all thy sons command." For those who may think the objection to the exclusionary nature of those lyrics is nothing but a twenty-first-century bout of political correctness, it should be noted that on the very day "O Canada" was made official back in 1980, the same concerns were raised. Ed Broadbent specifically singled out those lines for complaint in the speech he made supporting the bill. As did Florence Bird, the former chair of the Royal Commission on the Status of Women, that day in the Senate: "I also feel that true patriot love should be commanded in all of us and not just the sons of the country, because I assure you, honourable senators, I am nobody's son," she said. "Hear, hear," Hansard records her Senate colleagues saying in chastened response.

This one wasn't going to go away.

And so, starting in 1985, private member's bills to change "in all thy sons command" to "in all of us command" started appearing regularly on the order paper of the House. Two in 1985, one in 1986, another in 1987, and 1988, again in 1993, and 1994, nine bills in all. None of them succeeded. The movement took on new vigour in 2002, when senator Vivienne Poy launched a bill in support of the change, along with a spirited campaign. But it too was unsuccessful. And then, in 2010, the Conservative administration of Stephen Harper included this seemingly innocuous line in the Throne Speech opening that year's session of Parliament: "Our Government will also ask Parliament to examine the original gender-neutral English wording of the national anthem."

Hardly a revolutionary proposal, one would think. But the response to this potential change from Conservative voters was so aggrieved, so immediate and intense, that within forty-eight hours, a chastened government that was notorious for always sticking to its guns gave in and completely abandoned the proposal. The Conservatives were amazed that such a seemingly small issue could spark such major pushback. If they had studied previous attempts to change the anthem, perhaps they wouldn't have been surprised. But ever since, the Conservatives have considered changes to the anthem a political third rail.

But "in all thy sons command" continued to rankle. In 2013, a group called Restore Our Anthem—which included Vivienne Poy, former prime minister Kim Campbell, senator Nancy Ruth, and author Margaret Atwood—tried once again to promote the change. Their campaign received a great deal of attention. But the Conservative government was having none of it. Their near-death experience over the issue in 2010 had made them permanently gun-shy. Why expend so much political capital for such a small payoff? As 2014 approached, nearly thirty-four years after "O Canada" had become the official national anthem, "all thy sons" was still stubbornly holding its ground.

Then along came Mauril Bélanger. Bélanger had been a cabinet minister in Paul Martin's Liberal government and was MP for Ottawa–Vanier. In September of 2014, on the heels of the Restore Our Anthem campaign, Bélanger (then an opposition member) introduced a private member's bill to make the national anthem more gender inclusive. It was duly debated in the House in 2015 and, not unsurprisingly, defeated by the Conservative majority, although a few courageous Conservative members voted in favour of the measure.

But in October of 2015, the government changed hands—the Liberals had a majority, with another Trudeau as prime minister.

Bélanger tried again, reintroducing his bill, now called C-210, in January of 2016. By this time, sadly, he had been diagnosed with ALS, Lou Gehrig's disease, and the passage of his bill was inextricably intertwined with goodwill and support for him personally. When he introduced the bill for second reading in May, he had to use text-to-speech technology to formally propose it. With the support of the female-friendly government of Justin Trudeau, which had decided the time had come to make this change stick, Bill C-210, rare for a private member's bill, passed second reading in the House, took a very quick trip though the Commons heritage committee, and was back to the floor of the House for third reading on June 15, 2016. With Bélanger in the House one last time just weeks before his death, Bill C-210 was approved in a flurry of intense emotion. "O Canada" seemed ready to take on yet another incarnation.

But one more fight awaited, and a relatively nasty one at that—in, of all places, the Canadian Senate. Though the Senate had long been expected to simply rubber-stamp measures passed by the elected House of Commons, Justin Trudeau's government had recently introduced reforms to increase its independence and make it once again the chamber of "sober second thought" in the nation. This newly liberated Senate, or at least its Conservative members, decided to take a stand on a gender-neutral "O Canada." Part of their objection was procedural—they felt that the measure had been railroaded through the House by taking advantage of Mauril Bélanger's illness. Part of it was strategic, to give them bargaining power over other pieces of legislation. But there was an element that was undoubtedly political—they felt, not necessarily incorrectly, that many people in the country were against the idea of changing the lyrics. Based on these objections, it took the Senate a year and a half to approve Bill C-210. It was stalled at third reading for almost a year before it finally passed. The Senate gave its approval in January of 2018 and the bill received royal assent shortly thereafter. Finally, a thirty-eight-year saga—if not a century old one—had ended, and "O Canada" recovered its original gender neutrality. "In all of us command" is now part of the official lyrics of the anthem.

For the words of "O Canada" to be the site of such vigorous political battles may be surprising to some and seem foolish to many, but the struggle is completely understandable. An anthem defines many things about a nation—who we are, what we believe, who we would like to be, who we believe we were in the past. It is a backdrop for our political life, with the understanding that the life we share with others—past, present, and future—is the most important one we have. We need symbols to unify us as a community, but that search for unity is not always easy, especially in a contemporary world full of complexity, contradiction, and continuing evolution. Little stays as fixed as we would like it to these days—so it's no surprise that our national anthem keeps transforming itself as the country does the same.

THIRTEEN

THE CORTÈGE MADE ITS WAY slowly, deliberately, from the train station and across the Harbour Bridge.

Thousands lined the route as the hearse carefully descended into Montreal.

As it glided to a stop, bandleader Edmond Hardy lifted his arms, and 195 musicians began playing—solemnly, as it was always intended to be played—"O Canada."

Calixa Lavallée had finally come home.

Forty-two years after Lavallée's burial in Mount Benedict Cemetery in Boston, his remains had been returned to Montreal. It was July 13, 1933. After a public procession that included police officers, firemen, bands, and family members, with thousands of spectators lining the route, his body lay in state at the Notre-Dame Church (now Basilica). An elaborate funeral service was held the next day. "O Canada" sounded out several times during the two days of festivities and honours bestowed on the now-famous composer. For a week, media in Quebec and the rest of Canada had been transfixed by Lavallée's return. The papers were full of stories of his achievements. The fledgling Canadian Radio Broadcasting Commission, the forerunner to the CBC, broadcast tributes on its radio stations across the nation. It was the final chapter in the wandering minstrel's journey. On July 14, his body was re-interred in the Notre-Dame-des-Neiges Cemetery on Mount Royal, placing Lavallée high above the city that had nurtured him, applauded him, scorned him.

Lavallée's return to Quebec, as the Great Depression was ravaging that impoverished province, was driven by a powerful form of conservative French Canadian nationalism that had resurfaced in the 1930s. Like so many other peoples devastated by the collapse of the international economy during the Depression, French Canadians of that period tended to rally around the familiar. This was not the time for experimentation in political affairs. Or generosity. It was a time for retrenchment, for fearfulness, for regrouping. Within three years of Lavallée's repatriation, Maurice Duplessis and his Union nationale would take power in Quebec, beginning what many have called the Great Darkness in that province. The more nuanced French Canadian nationalism of a Henri Bourassa, the anti-clerical and anti-imperialist founder of *Le Devoir*, gave way to a more emotional, ecclesiastical, passionate national feeling associated with the figure of Abbé Lionel Groulx, one of the more controversial intellectuals of twentieth-century French Canadian history.

The proponents of this fervent right-wing nationalism felt a desire and need to reclaim Lavallée, to make him into a French Canadian hero. The thought of their native son languishing in a foreign land, he who had sung Quebec to itself, was intolerable. A proposed project to build a monument to Lavallée had foundered for lack of funds—the re-interment ceremonies were the next best thing.

In some ways, Lavallée's return to Quebec made of him a political puppet, just as he had been during his lifetime. For years after his repatriation, he was used as a symbol for nationalism in the province. His name and memory were revered in the 1930s, and even more so in the 1940s; it was in that decade that streets were named after him, the village where he was born was rechristened, and his memory was honoured throughout the province. Today, Lavallée's name is everywhere in Quebec. The little not-quite-a-town where he was born was officially made the municipality of Calixa-Lavallée in the 1970s. There are two schools named after him in Montreal, and streets named after him in towns and cities all over Quebec—Montreal, Quebec City, Shawinigan, Magog, Boucherville, Repentigny—and even on the University of Ottawa campus.

However, as the Quiet Revolution of the early 1960s gave way to the causes of sovereignty and separation in the later part of that decade and beyond, Lavallée and specifically "O Canada" became something of a cultural anomaly in Quebec. English Canada's embrace of Lavallée's tune seemed like the worst sort of cultural appropriation to the radicals in the province, especially since the original was so fervently dedicated to Quebec nationalism. The more English Canada embraced the anthem, the less Quebec was interested in it. And, of course, the ultra-conservative lyrics of Adolphe Routhier that celebrated the uncritical and indissoluble bond between the Church and *la patrie* struck modern Quebec as antiquated, to say the least, and for many served as a reminder of dark times in the province's history. If "O Canada" hadn't been sung every Saturday night, in lusty, full baritone voice by Roger Doucet at the Montreal Forum before Canadiens games, the song may not have survived the 1970s in Quebec.

Modern French Canada thus needed something other than "O Canada" to express its individuality and patriotism, and it turned to Québécois folksingers for inspiration. In 1966, the Saint-Jean-Baptiste Society awarded the most famous of these, Gilles Vigneault, a music prize named for Calixa Lavallée—an ironic twist, as it was Vigneault who would eventually write the song that would dethrone "O Canada" as the unofficial anthem of French Canada ("Gens du pays," the song that René Lévesque sang in defeat on referendum night in 1980). Today, "O Canada" exists in an uneasy place in modern Quebec, neither forgotten nor honoured. Every so often, the Saint-Jean-Baptiste Society suggests a new competition for a Quebec national hymn, but the idea seldom gathers much momentum. "O Canada" exists in a half-light in the province where it was born and for which it was written.

And Calixa Lavallée seems also to be stuck in the shadows, forgotten by history, at least in Quebec. In the rest of the country, we haven't forgotten him because we never knew he existed in the first place—a testament to the divide that still exists between French and English Canada. We still know very little about each other. However, since the near miss of the second Quebec referendum in 1995, sovereignty has been gradually fading as a rallying cry and as a viable political option for Quebecers, and managing the relationship between French and English Canada has consequently become less of a political tripwire in the past few years. We seem to have moved on as a country to other, more pressing issues in the first quarter of the twenty-first century, without ever really having resolved the bicultural conflicts that lay at the heart of our national political life for more than two centuries. So Lavallée stands less as a symbol of our country today than he might otherwise have been.

But when we think of Lavallée in his own terms and placed within his own times, both as a man and as a musician, what is most striking about him is that not until now, with the increasing scholarship devoted to his life and work, have we been able to see him as he saw himself, as a complete figure. No one, perhaps with the elusive Josephine as an exception, knew everything about

Lavallée during his lifetime. His Quebec colleagues, watching him fight for a national conservatory or perform with great virtuosity, were completely unaware of his life as a successful minstrel performer. His minstrel colleagues could not have known he had written two operas and studied serious music in Paris. His Parisian friends would have been in the dark about his North American experiences. His Quebec friends would have been surprised by his efforts as an advocate for American music and composers. He likely didn't tell his American compatriots that he had written a national hymn for French Canada. Audiences listening to him play Mendelssohn with the Boston Symphony Orchestra might not have been aware he was born in Canada at all.

No one but Lavallée knew his whole story, and this was no accident. Lavallée spent a good deal of his career reinventing himself, suppressing details of earlier lives as he took on new ones. One can only imagine that this fractured and incomplete life, as modern as it might seem today, caused the composer more than a little distress and made him a lonely man—someone who could confide in no one, who was understood and fully accepted by no one, who had only himself as a true companion.

It is easy to cast Lavallée as a tragic figure. Here was a man who spent a decade and a half wrenching himself out of the seductive world of minstrelsy, with its glamour and excitement and fame, to remake himself as a serious musician, only to find that his native country was relatively uninterested in his transformation— aside from its willingness to use his talents to further political and cultural ends not of his choosing. His story ends in exile from the land he so cherished.

But to cast Lavallée in this light is too easy and too simple-minded. It ignores the fact that his life was full of a great deal more success than failure. A lauded child prodigy; a man right at the heart of a fabulous entertainment business, whatever we may think of its morality; a teenager caught up in the midst of the Civil War; a student in Paris; a respected figure in his own society; a musical leader in his adopted one. A man always right in the middle of the action. It was a life of achievement and of excitement, even of glamour, built on a restlessness that became all-consuming.

If Calixa Lavallée is a tragic figure, it's because all Canadians are. We as a country weren't quite ready for him, even though he was ready for us, ready to lead us. He appeared in the world before his time and spent his life trying to bring everyone else along with him—often with success, but not always with the support he hoped for. Artists are by definition self-motivated and resourceful, but they need others to help them avoid the solitary darkness of their own creative imaginations. Lavallée didn't always find that light.

Even his fluid national feeling, his connection to both Canada and the United States, was misunderstood. We forget that the concept of nationalism that we know today was just in the process of gestation during Lavallée's lifetime. Ties of culture, language, ethnicity, and kinship were all more greatly valued than political nationhood when Lavallée came into the world in the 1840s. He was in his mid-twenties before the idea of Canada as a sea-to-sea Dominion was even suggested; the notion was too foreign to him to ever be an enterprise that was going to fire his creative and political imagination. But well into his adulthood, Germany wasn't a country yet, either. Nor was Italy. Even the United States, one could argue, wasn't a true nation until it had been transformed by the Civil War. (American historian Shelby Foote has said, in stunning simplicity, that before the Civil War people said, "The United States are . . ." After the war, they said, "The United States is . . ."

A more complete understanding of the effect of the conflict would be hard to come by.)

So for Lavallée, the ties that bound him were not ties of political nationality but of culture and ethnicity—his French Canadianness. And even then, the sense of nationhood that this inspired was sophisticated and subtle. Lavallée lived most of his life in English—during his minstrel career, in the war, in Boston during the last ten years of his life—but that doesn't seem to have been a major contributing factor to his sense of self and identity. He understood himself as a French Canadian all his life, even as he travelled outside of that culture and interacted on a much wider plane than most of his compatriots. But when the opportunity came to return to Quebec to contribute to his own society, he took it eagerly. One assumes that, even with his persistent wanderlust, if Quebec had been a little more welcoming to him between 1875 and 1880, he would have remained there for the rest of his life. But it wasn't, and Lavallée in the end became a model for the Canadian more honoured abroad than at home, a model that is only now losing its force in the world. But his loyalty was always to his countrymen and women, to the people with whom he shared a past and a present.

And what of Lavallée's *chant national*—what of "O Canada"?

Lavallée would surely be surprised to learn that his little tune is still being sung almost a century and a half after he wrote it. He would likely be shocked that it was torn out of its original cultural moorings and adopted by a nation that hardly existed in his lifetime. Whether he would approve of the fact that people now use his anthem to express their emotional attachment to a country he did not know, and did not especially understand or like, is an open question. Personally, I think he would be enormously pleased. A man who believed that music should create community and civic pride, even civic virtue, would appreciate seeing that his song had done just that. By various twists and turns, Lavallée has achieved exactly what he hoped to with "O Canada." It is an anthem that allows people to hear reflected in it their loftiest goals and most sublime emotions. Not bad for two minutes of music.

And what to make of the nationalism the song expresses? Does it really have any place in a modern, interconnected, omni-cultural world? Is "O Canada" anything other than an overused, tired bit of propaganda we've had around forever? If you want one answer to that question, attend one of the innumerable citizenship ceremonies held almost daily across the country. The singing of "O Canada" comes at the very end of the proceedings, just min-utes after Canada's newest citizens have received their certificates, sworn their oaths, faced their new future. And then, usually with the help of immigration officials discreetly stationed in the room, these Canadians tentatively, perhaps for the first time, sing of their "home and native land," people who moments ago were citizens of Greece, Sri Lanka, Ireland, Somalia, Afghanistan, the United States, Colombia, Guyana, Ghana—or any of countless other nations. Now they are Canadian, and singing "O Canada" is one of their very first acts as citizens. It means something to them, however hesitant they are, because the country they have just joined means something to them.

If there's a value to nationalism these days, that's what it looks like. Not strident and belligerent and bellicose, but modest and tentative and quiet—an understanding that the desire to create community is a powerful natural instinct and that a people can manufacture and embrace shared values, ideals that help them connect, support each other, and become larger and more expan-sive than they would have been on their own. When "O Canada" works as a patriotic hymn, it works on that level. Or should.

And perhaps now that "O Canada" has once again recovered its gender neutrality, its 138-year quest to be an accurate reflection of our country is over. Maybe now, as we approach the second quarter of the twenty-first century, this anthem from the nineteenth century has finally reached closure and has become what we want it to become. Maybe now it can sail into the future on untroubled waters. Somehow, however, I doubt it. The country continues to develop—maybe it is the twenty-second century that will belong to Canada—and the anthem likely will as well.

"O Canada" is important to us because it stands for something greater than we are, something which defines us. In its melody and words, we hear ourselves reflected. And perhaps most importantly, because song is a communal enterprise, we sing ourselves into being each time we perform it together. With each rendition of "O Canada," we renew the bonds of country and community. Calixa Lavallée, the artist who believed in music's ability to create civic value and virtue, would be satisfied.

A NOTE ON SOURCES

FOR THE LONGEST TIME, the only book-length biography of Calixa Lavallée was Eugene Lapierre's *Calixa Lavallée: musicien national du Canada*, written in 1936, revised in 1950 and 1966. Lapierre was a true champion of Lavallée's—he was behind the project to repatriate the composer's remains in 1933—but his book is full of factual errors and omissions, which have nonetheless unknowingly been repeated by many other writers.

All that changed in 2015 with the publication of Brian Christopher Thompson's meticulously researched volume *Anthems and Minstrel Shows: The Life and Times of Calixa Lavallée*. By examining in detail both Canadian and American newspaper sources from Lavallée's lifetime, Thompson was able to build up a comprehensive and considerably more accurate account of Lavallée's actual life than had ever existed before. In particular, Thompson revealed in depth Lavallée's minstrel career, setting a record straight that had been crooked and disguised for over a century. This volume was informed in large measure by Thompson's work. By and large, the English translations of French-language reviews of Lavallée's performances cited in this book are Thompson's.

The *Canadian Encyclopedia* online and several Government of Canada websites about Lavallée and "O Canada" also provided valuable information about the anthem and its composer, although many sources continue to include some of the errors in Lavallée's biography corrected by Brian Thompson's *Anthems and Minstrel Shows*.

There are a number of excellent histories and cultural critiques of minstrelsy, most written in the last thirty years. Dale Cockrell's *Demons of Disorder: Early Blackface Minstrels and Their World* puts the earliest days of minstrelsy into their true subversive context. Robert Toll's *Blacking Up: The Minstrel Show in Nineteenth-Century America* gives more of a historical perspective, while William Mahar's *Behind the Burnt Cork Mask: Early Blackface Minstrelsy and Antebellum American Popular Culture* combines analysis and history in equal measure. Finally, Eric Lott's *Love and Theft: Blackface Minstrelsy and the American Working Class* has the distinction of not only being a fine and nuanced analysis of minstrelsy and early industrialization—its title was borrowed by Bob Dylan for one of his albums.

The single best book about the Battle of Antietam is *Landscape Turned Red: The Battle of Antietam* by Stephen S. Sears. The National Park Service, which operates the Antietam battlefield as a National Historic Site, also has a great deal of detailed material on the battle. And if you're interested, YouTube has many video explorations of the Antietam battle, including several of the Antietam Memorial Illumination, when—every December—23,110 candles are lit on the battlefield site at dusk to commemorate the soldiers who were killed and wounded on that horrific day in September 1862.

There are a number of books about the musicians of the Civil War. Especially interesting are *Bands and Drummer Boys of the Civil*

War by Arthur Wise and Francis A. Lord and *A Pictorial History of Civil War Era Musical Instruments and Military Bands* by Robert Garofalo and Mark Elrod, which my guide at Antietam was convinced contained a previously unattributed picture of Lavallée as a Civil War bandsman. He may well be right—the picture in question is of two saxhorn players of the band of the Fourth Rhode Island, Lavallée's instrument and regiment. If it is not Lavallée himself in the picture, it is certainly two of his colleagues in the band.

To complete the Civil War references, John Boyko's *Blood and Daring: How Canada Fought the American Civil War and Forged a Nation* is a thorough—and thoroughly entertaining—look at Canada's impact on the Civil War and vice versa.

There are many fine volumes in English detailing French Canadian history and culture in the period of Lavallée's time in the province. Donald Creighton's *The Empire of the St. Lawrence* remains one of the great volumes of Canadian history, in which the hypothesis of a natural Canadian geographical continuity is explored and argued convincingly. Even though Creighton provides his historical examination of Quebec almost exclusively through the eyes of the English merchant class, it is still of considerable value. A.I. Silver's *The French-Canadian Idea of Confederation 1864–1900* provides a more detailed and sympathetic examination of French Canadian public opinion in the years preceding Confederation, and the several volumes of essays by historian Ramsay Cook, although tilted towards a federalist sympathy, are also illuminating. Lord Durham's report, often cited, seldom read, is available online in its original version. It deserves attention.

There are few sources of detailed information about Lavallée's time in Paris, but there is one superb volume that details the use of music to reconstruct French society after the disasters brought upon it by the Franco-Prussian War. *Composing the Citizen: Music as Public Utility in Third Republic France* by Jann Pasler is an 800-page examination of the use of music to forge a national consciousness at exactly the time Lavallée was in the French capital.

The online *Canadian Encyclopedia* article was the single best source I could find about the history of the English lyrics to "O Canada," and I was very impressed by the online accessibility and organization of the Debates of the House and Commons and Senate. Those debates are well worth an examination, for the drama and history that lurk just beneath the decorum and conventionality of discourse in Canada's Parliament.

And finally, because the Internet is not all bad, not all trolls and fake news, the original sheet music of Arthur Sullivan's "Dominion Hymn," lost for more than a century, is available online at https://archive.org/stream/CSM_001997#page/n1/mode/2up.